Fresh Cuts

Edwina von Gal

PHOTOGRAPHS
by John M. Hall

FOREWORD
by Ken Druse

 New York

Fresh Cuts

Unexpected Arrangements
with Branches, Buds, and Blooms

Text copyright © 1997 Edwina von Gal
Photographs © 1997 John M. Hall

Published in 1997 by Artisan
A Division of Workman Publishing Company, Inc.
708 Broadway, New York, NY 10003-9555
www.artisanbooks.com

Library of Congress Cataloging-in-Publication Data
Von Gal, Edwina
    Fresh Cuts : unexpected arrangements with
branches, buds, and blooms /
Edwina von Gal : photographs by John M. Hall
         p.   cm.
    Includes bibliographical references
    ISBN 1-57965-266-2
    I. Flower arrangement. I. Title.

SB449.V66   1997   96-47966
745.92--dc21   CIP

Printed in Spain

10 9 8 7 6 5 4 3 2 1
First paperback edition, 2004

Designed by Jim Wageman

Typefaces used in this book are Avenir,
designed by Adrian Frutiger, and Bauer Bodoni,
based on designs of Giambattista Bodoni.

DEDICATED

to the memory of Marjorie Vreeland von Gal,
my grandmother, and Peter Jay Sharp, my
mentor —EvG

to my grandmothers: Mama Hall, Ma Horner,
and Grannie Minnie —JMH

ACKNOWLEDGMENTS

With big thanks to the people who let us
use their homes for our pictures: Harry
Schnaper, John Waddell, Tom Flynn,
Mark McDonald, Gansevoort Gallery,
Terren Greene, Caroline and Jamie Curtis,
and Randall Sharp. To those who provided
technical assistance: Margaret Falk of the
New York Botanical Garden, Brent Heath
of the Daffodil Mart, and William Brumback
of the New England Wildflower Society/
Garden in the Woods. For kindness,
patience, talent, and amazing faith in a first-
time author: Leslie Stoker and Jim Wageman.
For support and friendship: Lynne Alvarez,
Anna McDonald, Bob Rumsey, Jim Osborne,
Joe Tyree, Christopher Smallwood, and
my daughter Ariel. —EvG

My many thanks to the above mentioned
whose spaces we used as locations,
especially John Waddell. To Garance Aufaure,
who inspired the means of which this book
is an end. To you, dear Edwina: we connected
at an opportune moment, and what a world
you opened. Thank you, Leslie Stoker, for
taking a chance on an idea that doesn't
quite fit into any easy category, and
Jim Wageman for understanding and making
it work visually. You both have been a dream
to work with. My deepest appreciation to
the staff at Artisan for their time and energy.
—JMH

Contents

Foreword

LATELY, I find that when I plan a garden bed or border, I don't think about flowers. Although color is paramount, flowers are often an afterthought. The more I garden, the less interest I have in flowers used as a chorus—massed in perennial borders or annual parterres. I tend to focus on the individual flower or plant form and color. Rather than glory in a broad swath of color, I prefer the solo performance of a woodland jack-in-the-pulpit; the simple gesture of its hooded spathe articulates nature's artistry. I have also become finicky about flower arrangements. Although I love voluptuous peonies and armfuls of fragrant lilacs, cinnamon fern crosiers in a tiny vase can give me just as much pleasure. When one looks closely at the botanicals in the backyard and beyond, a new world unfolds, one that goes well beyond the fleeting burst of a flower's hue to the more enduring and, in many ways, more intriguing world of seed pods in a vase or chunks of bark in a bowl.

In *Fresh Cuts*, landscape designer Edwina von Gal and photographer John M. Hall have taken on the challenge of disclosing some of the aesthetic secrets of the botanical kingdom. This writer/photographer team celebrates the commonplace: flower buds, twigs, stems, faded blossoms, and tiny fruits. We would all see these things if we only lingered a moment to take a second glance.

Color photography rarely gets a second chance. But von Gal and Hall have done much more than create events to be recorded and reproduced. They have made arrangements in selected locations and then subtly tweaked the presentation. Things as ill-favored as oak galls, when placed at the center of seven circles, are elevated from trimmings for the fireplace to objects for contemplation. In another instance, a conventional display of tulips in a glass cylinder becomes surreal. We are left to gaze at plump green tulip fruits instead of the usual flamboyant petals. Hall also creates abstractions with his use of light. A peaceful room is nearly disrupted by a shadow slicing through the formal setting. Another photograph shows ghostly leaves in a pale, botanical heaven. These are the leaves of summers past reduced to their fibrous essence.

Discovering the essence of a cut plant is intrinsic to the Japanese flower arranging discipline, *ikebana*, but in a different way, emphasizing line and form over substance. The Asian influence in *Fresh Cuts* is evident, although the gathered cuttings are never subjugated to strict rules of design. The arrangements conform to the vogue for minimalism, but they are timeless in their expression of essentials. While this honesty and simplicity again nods to the East, von Gal and Hall are always true to their subjects. Sturdy reeds speak for themselves. A brilliant tomato-red orb is suspended in a faceted cage of gold filigree. Fortunately, you are not left to wonder about these remarkable examples of vegetation. The plants above, for instance, are *Equisetum hymale*, horsetail, and *Physalis alkekengi*, Chinese lantern.

Von Gal introduces each species in straightforward captions, including Latin genus and species names. She goes on to embellish these facts with personal observations, memories, and literary references. Fat stems remind her of childhood delicacies such as celery stalks stuffed with peanut butter. She shares a modern legend about burdock, saying, "Velcro was invented by a shepherd inspired by burrs on his sheep." But what is more amazing to me is the choice of container. The spiky, sea anemone–like burrs are nestled in an iridescent shell. The paring of container to content is perfect. In another photograph, a thick crystal vase holds a vegetable. The red Swiss chard, with translucent stalks and veins, looks like stained glass.

The location is not included in the photograph of the Swiss chard. Yet the light suggests a room with a sunny window. In other photos, we see the rooms—spare and formal; I felt as if I should be quiet and respectful, as I would be in a library or museum. These images are a bit disquieting, but also challenging. I wanted to play a game: Who lives here? Have they just left the room, or are they about to return? There is a voyeuristic side to perusing these pages.

The accoutrements sprinkled about the compositions reiterate the presence of people just out of view: the contents of a turned out pocket, empty chairs, a well-worn book. These are so perfectly considered that they also work for the art of the illusion. Readers who share this glorious book are welcomed into these conjured settings—to become the temporary inhabitants of the authors' vision.

Fresh Cuts is a book about arranging parts of plants and flowers. But the compositions, the light, the facts and eccentricities, the book's design, and its remarkable attention to detail set it apart from the usual and expected. Like good painting and sculpture, this book will reward you with something different every time you look at it.

As I write this, I am looking at a vase on my desk stuffed with the dried stems of *Lilium formosanum*, which branch like candelabras topped by four-inch-tall seed pods. I know that some fascinating flower or branch or other kind of vegetation can be collected in the garden in every month of the year to bring inside for decoration and enjoyment. *Fresh Cuts* introduces this original notion, and offers a different view of the natural world. Most of the cuttings in this book are not made of fresh flowers, but fresh ideas.

Ken Druse
January 1997

Introduction

ALTHOUGH it may seem peculiar to amuse oneself with reading *Stearn's Dictionary of Plant Names for Gardeners* or *An Illustrated Flora of the Northern United States and Canada,* it is a form of fun for people who are fond of plants. Reading botanical reference works is the same for me as taking a walk in my own neighborhood, or spending a long time with someone I know: it offers unexpected insights from familiar sources. We plant-lovers understand that a knowledge of plants provides a good deal more than amusement; mine has given me employment (as a landscape designer), moments of serenity, and the opportunity to participate actively in the symbiotic relationship between plants and animals.

Horticultural knowledge is customarily pursued through study and gardening and questioning. Another avenue—one not so obvious to the uninitiated—is flower arranging. To me, flower arranging involves a lot more than flowers, and much more than arranging, but I can't find a better name for it. It is a simple, cyclical process: first, go outdoors, anywhere, and look closely at every bit of plant life around to discover something that is beautiful or interesting. This could be any part of a plant: bark, branches, buds, pods, leaves, weeds, seeds, or flowers—alive or dead. Take it home with you. Step two is selecting the perfect container—one that is complementary in size, shape, and color—and then making a bouquet that best displays the object of your interest. Next, place it in a spot where it will catch your attention and make you pause a second, or where you can stare at it while doing something else. Notice how it changes as time passes. If you don't know what it is, look it up. If you do know, look at it so closely that you see something in it that you never saw before. Next time you see it again outdoors, notice where it comes from: the process is complete and beginning over.

Flower arranging is not necessarily an exclusive or elusive pastime. It can cost nothing. It need not take much time. It makes you feel good. It is an accessible path to a deeper knowledge of plants.

notes on collecting plants

It is especially important to follow the code of ethics that is recognized by horticulturists for picking plants in the wild. First, be sure you know what and where you are picking. Never pick an endangered species, and get permission from the landowner before removing any plants. Also, know how and how much to cut. Always cut to improve the shape and health of a plant, never take more than ten percent of a plant or plant population, and leave little or no evidence of your cutting.

Part 1
Body

Body: The Logic and Beauty

PLANTS HAVE BEEN a major source of inspiration for artists since
art began, and even after all that time no one complains that they have
become irrelevant. Looking closely at the way familiar plants are
structured reveals how much we have missed while thinking that we
"know" them. One of the biggest leaps in my education as a gardener
came with the realization that the key to success is keen observation.

of Form

L e a f   B u d s

Acer Larix kaempferi
Japanese larch

OPPOSITE

Fagus sylvatica
European beech

Buds are a big part of a tree's identity. They contain the next year's leaves, flowers, and twigs. They say some things that the leaves don't. A while ago, when I was but a bud myself in my life with plants, I made the mistake of confusing *Acer platanoides* (Norway maple) with *Acer saccharum* (sugar maple). This is no way to impress a nurseryman. So I learned that although their leaves are somewhat similar, the terminal buds (on the twig ends) of these two maples are not. Those of the Norway are much larger and greener. This completely personalizes its silhouette. You just have to know where to look.

Each species of tree has a unique type of bud. The bud's size, shape, texture, and place of attachment all provide basic information for identification. Within each bud and its bit of branch is stored the food it will need to commence growth in the spring. If conditions were good the previous summer there will be a reserve, making that plant less vulnerable to any harsh conditions come spring.

The spot where a lateral bud (on the twig side) forms is called a node; the space between buds is an internode. The internodes mark growth achieved in the previous season. The length of the internodes indicates how good a year it was: If the plant is healthy, with good reserves, the growth will be correspondingly robust. Newly transplanted or stressed trees have very short internodes. Thus a plant's history is written in internodes as well as in the trunk's rings.

Now that I know they have so much to tell me, I look hard at buds. But when I cut branches and force them I am still not always sure which buds will produce the leaves and which the flowers.

Without realizing it, most people share a misconception about how trees grow. You assume that a tree grows up all over, like a child. You imagine that a little branch low on a sapling will some day be the same big branch, high enough to hold a swing. But you also know that, once hung, the swing will always hang at the same height. In fact, a branch always remains the same distance off the ground from the moment it is born. On most trees, if a lower limb is damaged or removed, the tree will not replace it. New branches are formed on the twigs where the buds are.

Leaves

Ligustrum ovalifolium
California privet

There are moments in my learning process that make me both elated and embarrassed, revelations that forever change my perception but that are so simple and so obvious it is hard to admit to the blind ignorance that preceded them. I call them my "little epiphanies." I had one when at last I understood the essence of plant morphology (i.e., anatomy). To know one plant from another an initiate checks the fine detailing as well as the architecture. Do the leaves and twigs emerge directly opposite one another along a branch, like wings, or do they appear in a more random, alternate pattern?

There are practical applications. Littleleaf hollies can look very much like boxwoods, but boxwoods grow very slowly and live longer, making them far more expensive. When shopping for plants, I can't be fooled. I know boxwoods are opposite and hollies are alternate.

Because there are fewer opposite than alternate plants, it is easier to remember the opposites. One easy mnemonic for memorizing the most common opposite trees is to think "MAD" for maple, ash, and dogwood.

Privet is opposite. I have a theory that that is one of the reasons it makes such a good hedge. Just below every spot where you prune there are two leaves instead of one. When a privet hedge is newly planted it looks new, thin and awkward, so it is fed and watered to encourage rapid growth. Once it reaches its desired height and thickness it has no idea it is supposed to stop. From then on it must be cut once or twice a year, forever, providing an endless oversupply of greens for arrangements.

Hydrangea quercifolia, Polygonatum odoratum 'Variegatum', Poa pratensis
oakleaf hydrangea, Japanese Solomon's seal, bluegrass

Emerging leaves, fresh from their bud wombs, are living off stored sugars and have not yet developed their capacities for photosynthesis, or survival. They have the appeal of babies, pale and tender. They appeal to people who prefer emerging slowly from winter. They perform a quiet show for those of us who like to slowly acclimate our eyes to color as the sun gets stronger. I doubt that this kind of display will ever compete with the color-starved majority's beloved masses of red and yellow tulips, but competition is hardly in a young leaf's vocabulary, and that seems to me the essence of newborns and spring.

17

Matteuccia struthiopteris, Hosta
ostrich fern, hosta

People never fault nature's taste and sense of
style as they do one another's. Nature has
provided all the models for our aesthetics.
Ferns and hostas, for instance, have all the
attributes for a visually pleasing compo-
sition—the coarse texture and the fine, the
variation on a color theme, the vertical and
the horizontal—and they like the same habi-
tat. In nature, where hostas do not normally
occur, their place as fern companion is taken
by skunk cabbage. Perfect pairings like this
occur often in nature, and gardeners do
their best to copy them. As nature is irrevers-
ibly changed by man's clumsiness, perhaps
our aesthetics will follow and ease the pain.

Fern fronds emerge from the earth tightly
coiled. In their partly unfurled state they are
called fiddleheads. Eating fiddleheads is the
vegetable equivalent of dining on tiny roasted
birds like quail: naughty and delicious. Cutting them for flower arranging is just as difficult and seductive. Perhaps the reverence we
unanimously share for a young fern's beauty is
emphasized not just by its intense fragility but
by the fact that each one you cut means one
less frond in your garden, and we never get
our fill. Fronds hold well as cuts if they are
totally submerged in cool water for an hour
or so before arranging and the stems are not
recut. I plan to include ferns in my dream cutting garden, where I'll grow all sorts of plants
for their buds, leaves, twigs, and flowers—
all just for my amusement, admiration, and
education in the garden and in my house.

Hosta, Ligularia 'Desdemona'

A plant's leaves are its lungs. Water taken up by the roots is exhaled through the leaves. Once, when I was concerned about the health of a newly transplanted tree, I asked a knowledgeable horticulturist for his opinion. He reached into the tree, clasped some leaves between his palms, and diagnosed a likely demise. The leaves were warm. A healthy leaf is cool due to evaporation, he said. The tree had stopped breathing and it did die, and I fell in love with that man.

It might be that most people know the shapes of leaves from pictures rather than from plants. We are mostly oblivious to leaves; they exist as a part of something else, such as a tree, until they do something amazing, like turn orange. In the case of hostas and ligularias, the leaves are the whole plant. They both have flowers, but flowers come and go. They both react negatively to too much sun. It is true of many large leaves. It must be in the proportions, the small size of the root system versus an extra large transpiration surface. They hyperventilate and faint.

Cutting big leaves and plunking them deep into water keeps them fresh a long time, provided they are kept out of the sun. In a slanting light their textures are emphasized.

head of iceberg lettuce and a cabbage? Can you describe it? I read that question somewhere, and it has stuck with me. We always know the names of the things we eat, and, because everyone else knows them too, a more precisely descriptive vocabulary is not generally required. But it exists. First, there are the Latin names, consisting of genus and species. Genus describes related types, and species names an individual attribute. In addition, there is a large vocabulary of botanical adjectives to explain how it all looks.

Cabbage is in the genus *Brassica*, which also includes kale, broccoli, cauliflower, mustard, and others. Its species name, *oleracea*, means vegetable-like (there are some brassicas that don't look at all like food), and *capitata* means "leaves in a dense head." Cabbage is described by the Royal Horticultural Society *Dictionary of Gardening* as "*B. oleracea capitata*—lvs large, closely packed, fleshy, smooth, glaucous green, lyrate, undulate, terminal segment large, 5 lobed, blunt."

Lactuca (lettuce) is a genus with less variety in the related forms. The name *Lactuca* is derived from the word for milk, and much of the lettuce family has milky sap. *Sativa* simply means cultivated. "*L. sativa*—glabrous, rosulate leaves to 25 cm, undivided or runcinate-pinnatifid, shortly petiolate; stem lvs ovate to orbicular, simple, sessile, cordate, clasping."

And so botanical nomenclature might invade one's life, providing a whole new way of looking at your dinner, not to mention its effect on your dinner conversation.

Brassica oleracea capitata,
Lactuca sativa
cabbage, lettuce

A good deal of a person's perception of home has traditionally included the local flora. The more I know about the plants where I live the more I learn and the more I feel estranged in places with unfamiliar plants, compelling me to know them too . . . it could keep me amused forever.

Do you know the difference between a

OPPOSITE
Stachys byzantina
lamb's ears

Somewhere someone wrote that the reason Marilyn Monroe seemed to glow on film was that she was covered with a quantity of short, fine, blond hair . . . or fuzz . . . or fur? I've been making a list of all the botanical words I can find that describe different ways in which plants can be hairy: ciliate, comose, pubescent, stellate pubescent, hirsute, hirtellus, hispid, hispidulous, pilose, indumentose, puberulent, setose, sericeous, tomentose, tomentulose, villous. I think for Marilyn I would choose pubescent; when my daughter was born she was decidedly tomentose, and I must admit to a liberal cover of indumentum. Isn't it seventeen words that the Eskimos have for snow, and not one for war?

Typically, silver-haired plants are tolerant of drought. Apparently the silver reflects heat and the hairs reduce the evaporation rate.

This kind of clever adaptation takes place again and again throughout a drought-tolerant plant's vascular system, so it is not a surprise to find that they do not take very well to standing in water. I find that stachys can look good for a day or two in a vase. As the bottom leaves begin to go bad (the blossoms last longer), simply pull them off.

Magnolia grandiflora
southern magnolia
leaves and seed pods

Magnolia grandiflora is described as having pubescent buds and leaves with tomentose undersides. The seed pods, too, are fuzzy, remaining prominently displayed on branch tips long after the encircling cup of soft, smooth, pale cream petals have fallen. The added contrast of the hard, bright shine of the dark green leaves makes every part of this plant ideal for arrangements. One form has been selected, propagated, and marketed for the way its leaves twist up to reveal their ornamental undersides. Very *Seven Year Itch*.

*Chamaecyparis pisifera
filifera aurea variegata*
dwarf golden threadleaf
false-cypress

In addition to all the advantages that Latin names provide in terms of accuracy, there's the fun of using and saying them. The plant pictured here carries the first Latin name that my daughter learned, captivated by its silliness and undaunted by the concept of Latin or spelling or correct pronunciation at the age of six. Would you use it if you knew you could say it?

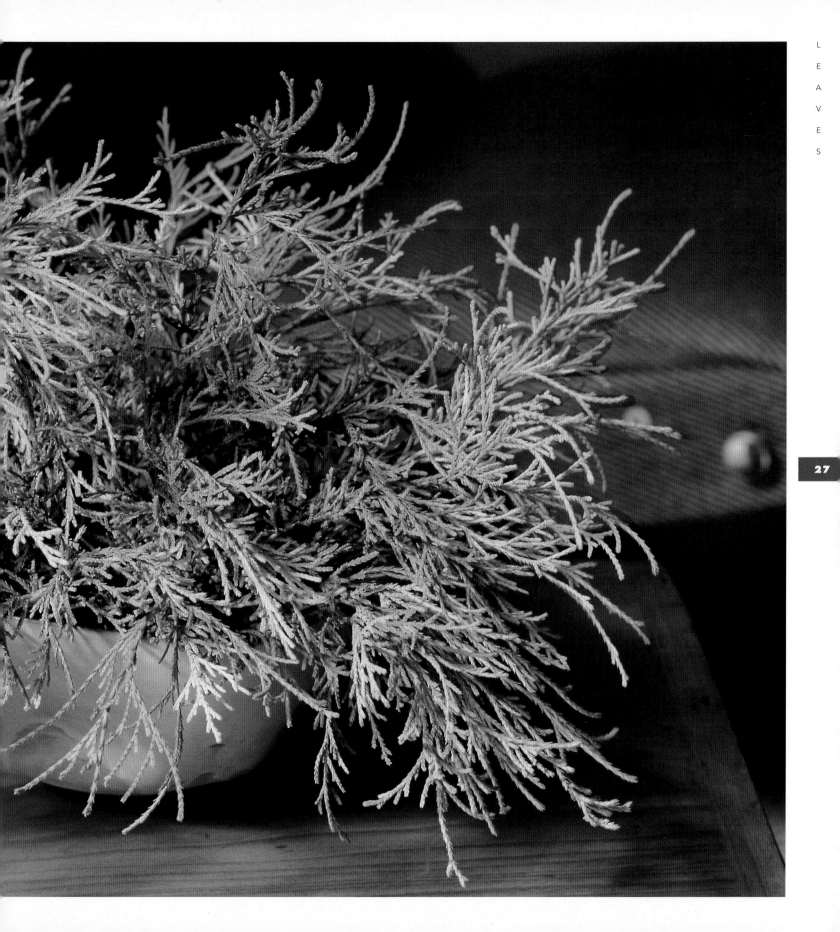

from your garden or the market, they provide an aromatic bouquet that is easily accessible for cooking. If they've been purchased or harvested with the roots still on, just rinse the leaves and stuff the whole bunch in water. The key is not to submerge any foliage: it will rot and speed deterioration. If you aren't eating them right away, most herbs will look presentable and remain useful for quite a while provided the water is changed every day and you keep them out of the sun.

OPPOSITE

Pinus thunbergii
Japanese black pine

When examined closely, pine needles are like pieces of hot dog sliced longitudinally like a pie. They occur in bundles of two, three, or five, depending on the species, the needles fitting neatly together to form a cylinder. The number of needles in a bundle never varies within most species, so needle count is a basic way to distinguish among pines. A plantsman once told me that species that share the same needle count often share the same cultural requirements and disease resistances. If a two-needled pine, say red pine, died of a disease in your yard it would be unwise to replace it with Austrian pine, another two-needled species.

Pines and other conifers grow needles on newly formed wood only. Most hold their needles for two years or so before dropping them. This means that the needles you see on a tree usually represent the last two years' growth. Because they stay on so long (as opposed to about six months for leaves on a deciduous tree) they are far more susceptible to an accumulation of any harmful elements in their air or water. As a result, evergreens are typically ill equipped for urban or polluted situations.

Rosmarinus officinalis, Ocimum basilicum 'Green Ruffles'
rosemary, basil

I pronounce herb with an audible "H." My mother always has—ever since she met the ladies of the Herb Society. It is the British pronunciation. And after all, what self-respecting Anglophilic gardener would drop her "aitches"? Although the aim in "hort talk" is always accuracy in identification, the pronunciations of botanical terms can be quite arbitrary; Americans don't always use the British form, and little of it is what an ancient Roman or Greek would have said. For names on which there is no consensus, or if you are just not sure, I recommend choosing one pronunciation and sticking with it in an authoritarian way.

Most herbs last well in winter. Whether

Phalaris arundinacea picta
ribbon grass

Ribbon grass, aka garter grass, aka invasive, spreads by roots and seed with such exuberance that you wonder why it has not taken over big chunks of countryside, as has the dreaded loosestrife. Something must hold it back. Perhaps not enough people have planted it in their gardens yet. That may be due to the fact that once it blooms it begins to look tired, floppy, and ratty. This is easily remedied by mowing it down just as the bloom spikes begin to appear in midsummer. A bit of extra water and it is a new plant in a week or so. I may be contributing to a new scourge.

The appeal of this phalaris is its variegation. The variegated (white) parts indicate a lack of chlorophyll and therefore reduced photosyn-thetic capability. As a result, variegated plants are usually the more noticeable but weaker forms of their species. If the all-green form of phalaris is even stronger, it is a good thing that it is too boring to be cultivated.

Acer
maple hybrid

Ever since my mother bought the house she lives in now, almost ten years ago, we have wondered about the strange and wonderful maple tree near the side door. No one seems to know exactly what its real name is. I have asked knowledgeable friends and so has Mom, but none of the possibilities suggested can be right. In the fall the leaves turn a brilliant red not displayed on the trees it otherwise resembles. I imagine it as the result of some fiery cross-pollination. Its shape is strangely, intriguingly irregular, too much so for it to have commercial potential. Growers do not appreciate gnarly limbs that swoop and dip, but a resident tree frog does.

OPPOSITE
Rhus typhina
staghorn sumac

There are three native sumacs that appear frequently on roadsides and empty lots. They are hard to distinguish from one another. The staghorn is the easiest to recognize: it consists of long, straight fuzzy stems that resemble new antlers. Its fruits hold longest into the winter, making staghorn the best sumac for cutting. It could be off-putting to know that it is cousin to both poison ivy and poison oak.

Houttuynia cordata 'Chameleon', Ampelopsis brevipendunculata
porcelain berry vine

Every aspect of a plant can inspire its own world of scientific study. Ask any simple question and it is probably being pursued through arenas within arenas of research prompting further questions, each attracting a group of people devoted to that study alone. Studies become more and more specific, perhaps obscure, but may ultimately emerge as highly relevant. A lot has been discovered lately about what causes the coloration in plants. It is outwardly simple, just sugars and reflected light, which of course is not simple at all. As with so many things learned from plants, a use will probably be found for this knowledge, most likely unrelated to the plant's agenda.

Houttuynia is called chameleon because of the color variations that occur from plant to plant, leaf to leaf, and from sun to shade. They mostly appear quite subtle when grown in shade, but in the sun, much more yellow is added to intensified reds.

Coccoloba uvifera
sea grape

A deep scientific knowledge of plants is not necessary to suggest uses for them other than as food. While lounging on a tropical beach, one might not realize that the nearby sea grapes produce an edible fruit. It is obvious, however, that the leaves make great plates for picnics. Sea grapes are one of the few plants that thrive on dunes in warm climates, so they are everywhere. Their presence is so strikingly ubiquitous that it was a surprise to me that there are 149 species of the genus *Coccoloba. Uvifera* is apparently the only one with such easily recognizable usefulness.

OPPOSITE

Fagus grandifolia
American beech

One of the first signs of spring for me is a remnant of the fall. Just before the big show begins, the last year's leaves of the understory beeches, which are still holding on, begin to glow. Looking into the woods, you see them distinctly. They have become diaphanous after a winter without any leaves on the trees above to protect them from the sun. The long angle of the light as spring approaches hits them in just the right way to capitalize on this skeletonization. They have all the weightlessness and command of the flowers to follow. The species name technically means large-leaved. The leaves are not really so large, but they are grand.

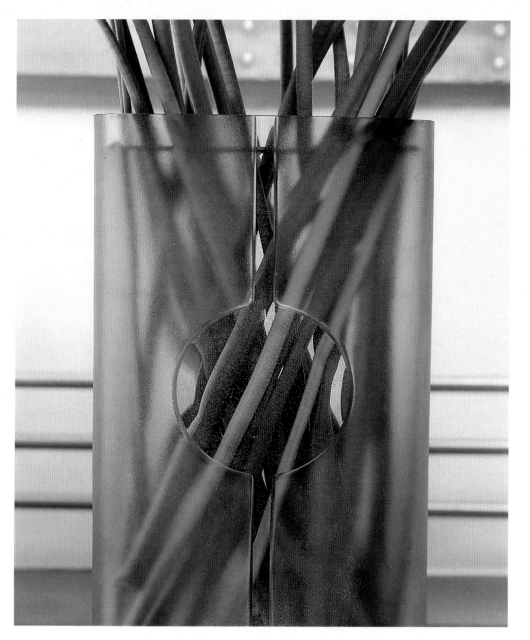

biennial, requiring two seasons of growth, with at least a month of cold winter in between, to trigger the seed-making process. The leaves can be harvested continuously throughout the summer and well into the cooler weather by cutting each stem near its base. In the fall the leaf color becomes darker and more complex. Not great with peanut butter, but delicious sauteed with shallots.

Anemone coronaria Mona Lisa group
florists' anemone

Making arrangements makes me study vases as well as what I put in them. Choosing the vase is an important part of the process: an exercise in balance and emphasis; a complementary mix of the sets and the performer. Now and then I find a container that really gets it. A vase with a plant dialogue. This one even kicked up a random dusty memory. Looking at these stems brought back a line from a Dylan Thomas poem: "The force that through the green fuse drives the flower / Drives my green age." Did Dylan Thomas garden? Certainly the designer of this vase made flower arrangements.

OPPOSITE
Beta vulgaris
rhubarb chard

When I was a child, one of my favorite science experiments was placing pieces of celery in a glass of tinted water to watch the dye rise up through their vascular systems. Before we feared red dye #2, the colored stalks made great snacks stuffed with peanut butter.

As opposed to red food coloring, the soil that produces my red chard is dark brown. Chard is an easy plant to grow, holding up through the heat of summer. It will not bolt (go to seed) like lettuce, which gets tough and bitter as a result. This is because it is a

Cornus sericea 'Silver and Gold'
variegated yellow-twig dogwood

Barry Ferguson, an extraordinary florist and gardener, once expressed to me his disinclination to prefer spring over the other seasons. Not what I expected from a man whose life is flowers and who has a passion for primroses, which are spring bloomers. Too easy, he said, too sweet, immature—"just like a pretty young thing in a prom dress." A good line, I thought. Now, some years later, I think he really meant it, and I am beginning to understand.

In my youth I found winter so cold and boring I promised myself I would spend my life (gardening) in a place with endless summer. A promise I am not keeping. What seemed then like the eternal emptiness of winter is now a reflection on negative space. While winter colors may be muted, there is a lot that is not subtle, like the cold and what a plant must do to endure it. Even after they have made their big fall adjustments, there is always plenty going on in the plant world to keep one amused. The pace is just slower, allowing for a more leisurely approach to observation and contemplation. I am not always ready for spring's frenetic pace.

The best color in yellow-twig dogwoods occurs in the winter on branches that grew during that year. Older wood turns gray-brown. When cut, the branches hold a long time in water, especially if you change it now and then. Any twigs remaining on the plant after winter cutting forays can be pruned to the ground in the spring, insuring a full head of all-new, brightly colored, straight stems to cut for the next winter. This method of pruning, called stooling, originally developed as a method of obtaining long, straight, pliable shoots from trees and shrubs such as willows for making baskets and the like. It keeps plants rounded and compact. It is certainly the easiest pruning method to describe.

A bonus for spring-hungry gardeners is cuttings that root. The shrub dogwoods do this well. Arrange some stems in a clear vase, wait a few weeks, and watch as roots develop at the nodes. The presence of light hinders this process, so it's best to keep them out of direct sun. As the roots grow, the twigs break dormancy, leaves will begin to form, and the yellow in the bark begins to change to its more greenish summer color. If the twigs are not planted or fertilized, the leaves will soon use up all of their stored sugars, and they will die.

Rubus occidentalis
black raspberry

Cutting plants with thorns is doubly difficult. In addition to the threat of the thorns piercing your fingers, they snag onto one another, making branches become frustratingly entan-

gled. This is why florists strip the thorns off roses, to slip them easily into a vase. This is surely why raspberries are not a more popular home garden item. In addition to the mysterious rituals of when and which and how much to prune, there is the impossibility of pulling the designated removals out of their patch.

I call these "ghost branches." They often grow in the woods, where the dim light causes them to grow individually rather than in dense clumps and their color is more apparent than in the sun. Their arching habit, which makes them so graceful in arrangements, is the way they renew themselves. When the tip bends back to touch the ground, it roots and grows a new cane. You might notice that all my branches had to be cut at both ends.

OPPOSITE
Malus
apple

When you are cutting for arrangements just before or during flowering, it is also a good time to prune. Shortly after it blooms, a plant begins to grow flower buds for the next year's display. Cutting thereafter will reduce the number of blossoms that will reach maturity, but midsummer is ideal to prevent excessive sucker growth. Cutting late in the growing season can also be detrimental if it encourages tender new growth that cannot tolerate summer sun or will not have time to grow tough enough for the winter. For some plants, pruning in the fall will cause them to die back where they have been cut. If you aren't sure, it is always safer to wait until dormancy has begun, after the time of the first frost. Wait a bit longer and you can force the blossoms.

Bark

tree bark (assorted)

They say if you are lost in the woods you can find north by noticing where the moss grows on tree trunks. The south side is sunny and hot; the north, shady and moist—moss territory. It is generally acknowledged that as a tree matures, its bark grows differently on the south side than on the north, to compensate for the diverse conditions. Therefore, when a tree is transplanted, it is important to note its north side and maintain its orientation. This is particularly pertinent to thin-skinned and older trees, with which I readily sympathize.

Bark covers trees with protective strength and individual style. It saves tree innards from attack and injury with a wide variety of textures and thicknesses. I was oddly delighted when I learned that in Indonesia bark is called "tree skin." When it is put that way it becomes so much harder to smack my lawn mower up close to a trunk for that last blade of grass; so much more interesting to watch, and help, a wound heal; so much easier to understand the frost cracks on the side that freezes and thaws in the bright winter sun.

In keeping with its toughness, bark does not decay as quickly as the "meat" of a tree does. It sometimes remains on the ground, retaining its shape where it falls, an empty exoskeleton. Birches do this especially well, which explains the canoes.

Quercus
oak galls

Bark is not a perfect armor. It is not always effective against all the attackers who want in, such as bacteria, fungi, viruses, nematodes, mites, and insects, all of which can cause the formation of galls. Galls are areas of increased size or quantity of cell growth; i.e., tumors. There are about 1500 varieties caused by insects alone, many of them wasps.

Galls become a nursery, food and shelter for the builders' offspring as well as for a succession of later, unrelated inhabitants. Sometimes newcomers arrive early and eat their accidental hosts, or their hatchlings do. Slicing and peering into a gall offers the queasy allure of a weird and beautiful horror film.

About 800 types of insect galls live on oaks—on the roots, trunk, branches, twigs, leaves, flowers, and fruit (acorns). They are sometimes so prevalent that they provide an easy way to identify oaks in winter.

The oak is a good host, apparently unfazed by all the activity. I have heard the galls called decorative, but I find them disturbing. Perhaps I don't really know about sharing. Do they itch?

winged. This is what close observation reveals: corky "wings" along each branch. Far more subtle than the "burning" leaves, the wings are certainly sufficiently prominent to give the plant a distinctive silhouette in winter.

Winged euonymus tends to grow in a densely haphazard fashion. It benefits a great deal from pruning out the weak, crossing, and inward-growing branches. The winter is the best time to do so; without the leaves, you can see what you are doing. The cuttings will last indefinitely in water and not quite as long without.

OPPOSITE

Pyrus communis var. *sativa*
e d i b l e   p e a r

I love pruning. My daughter says it is all about my need to control, "and she should know." Pruning is much like parenting, except that plants are a good deal more predictable and more easily controlled than children and can be ruled by logic. With plants experimentation and observation are the key, and the risks are not great. The basics seem complex at first, but practice and familiarity reveal their true simplicity. Leaves need sun and air. Pruning stimulates growth. Remove enough branches to allow light in but not so many that the photosynthetic capacity of the plant is reduced to below its minimum—never more than a third of a woody plant (unless you are coppicing or stooling, which should be done only in early spring and not on all plants). Always cut to a node or stem but not close enough to injure it. Step back a lot and look at what you've done.

Euonymus alatus
b u r n i n g   b u s h

Often the difference between the Latin and common names of a plant lies in how closely you are looking. "Burning bush," the common name, describes what most people see: a quiet shrub that bursts into flame-colored glory in the fall. In the Latin name, *alata* means

Roots

Salix alba 'Vitellina'
golden willow

A general assumption is that trees grow throughout the growing season. This is partly true, but not as you might think. Most of a tree's annual growth above the ground takes place within a few weeks after it leafs out in the late spring. This new growth must harden off in order to survive the challenges of drought, heat, and cold that lie ahead. Thereafter, new buds need to be set and food stored for the following spring. And then, after the leaves (or needles) drop in the fall, while the soil temperature remains above freezing, the roots, relieved of the considerable tasks put on them by the leaves, have their turn to do most of their growing. They will continue to do so, at rates proportionate to the soil temperature, until most of their energies must again be devoted to leaf and wood growth in the spring.

Willows are renowned for their roots. They are fabled for their avid search for water, causing them to invade and destroy drain pipes, septic systems, and damp basements. Willow branches root readily, so much so that eroding stream banks can be stabilized by poking them full of fresh-cut willow sticks, which will quickly grow a thick mat of soil-hugging roots. I could not possibly find a use for all the willow branches I have rooted, unless you count the pleasure it gives me.

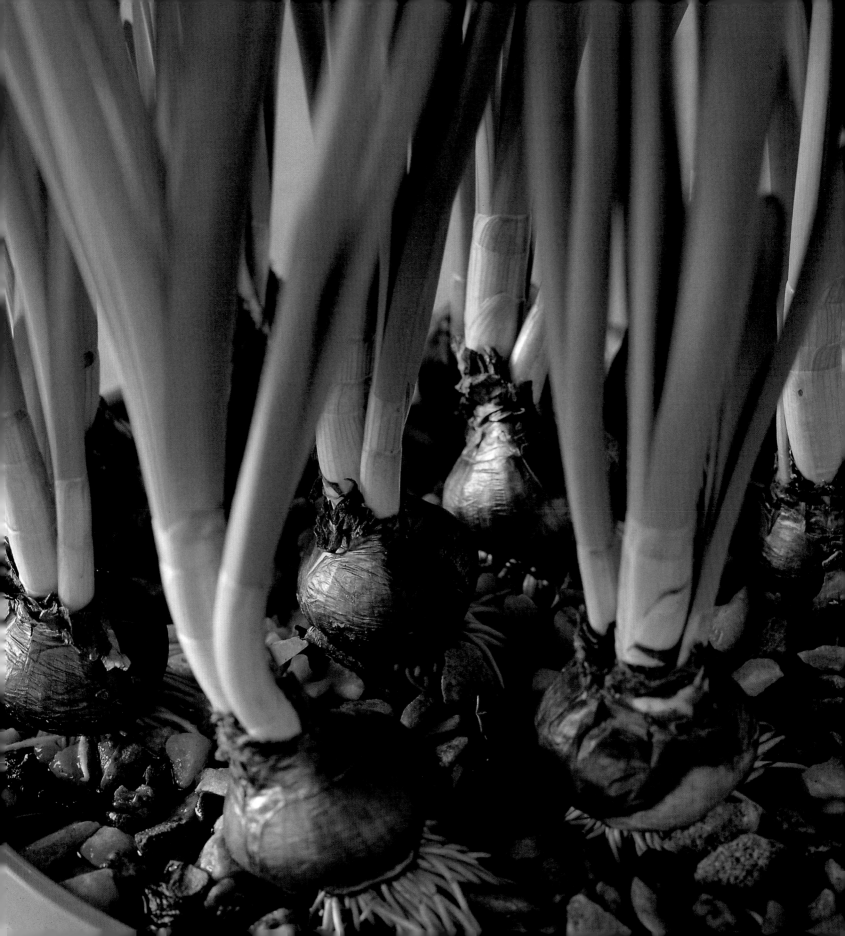

Narcissus tazetta
p a p e r w h i t e

The first year that many bulbs are planted,
they will generally bloom later than others
of their kind. I assume it is because they
have to grow roots and catch up with those
already in the ground. In addition, if planted
sideways, they will begin to turn over and
eventually right themselves. Many pull
themselves deeper into the soil. This is done
with contractile roots, which push down into
the soil and then expand and shorten, bring-
ing the bulb with them. I have seen bulbs
do this in soil that was so hard to dig that
the gardener (me) did not persist in planting
them deep enough. I am awed by the strength
it took for them to move and curious why the
ability to move has not evolved in other,
much easier, circumstances.

When narcissus bulbs are grown in a lot of
water their roots go wild. (Was it a reference
to this that inspired the story of the young
god Narcissus, eternally stuck to a riverbank?)
Without soil, the bulb is not nourished, and it
will be too weak to bloom the following year.

Part 2
Soul

Soul:
Fragility,
Invention,
Per

THE EXISTENCE of any living thing is predicated on its ability to survive long enough to reproduce and to reproduce enough to proliferate. The ability of a plant to defend itself against predators keeps it in the game long enough to produce flowers and then seeds. The ability of the flower to attract the appropriate pollinator at the right time will insure genetic diversity. The ability to produce sufficient quantities of viable seed and distribute them to places where they will thrive helps maintain a large enough population to repeat the process. As plants must do all this without moving, they have developed intricate dependencies on climate, soil, weather, insects, animals, and humans. They have learned to place themselves so as to obtain the food, water, and air they need, to attract insects and animals with their bright flowers and sweet pollen, and to entice humans with their beauty.

petuation

Anemone coronaria
Mona Lisa group
florists' anemone

One of my big heroes is Carolus Linnaeus. He was the botanist who developed the system of binomial nomenclature (genus and species) by which all plants are identified, the Linnaean system. There were many scientists working on developing a logical, universal method for classifying plants and animals. They tried using common characteristics of form to arrange similar plants into categories. Linnaeus used common characteristics of reproductive organs. His system won out. Sex sells.

In spite of their exhibitionist reproductive organ displays, or perhaps because of them, the luscious anemonies sold by florists are a product of the plant breeders' art, not the birds and the bees. Like other flowers that strut their stuff with such exuberance, they have attracted humans as their pollinators and protectors.

Lycopersicon esculentum var.
cerasiforme 'Sweet 100'
cherry tomato

We collect and revere the sex organs of plants—their flowers. Using them as the linking trait for organizing plants into an accurate and workable system of identification was a genius of logic. As much as matching similar leaves or bark might seem to indicate close familial ties, the flowers are where it really happens, where the generations are begun, the place of origin. Looking for similarities in flowers makes one begin to notice shared traits among seemingly dissimilar plants. The tomato flower is the one I noticed first in this respect. Actually, it was the nightshade, the nightshade vine that grew at the edge of the woods adjacent to my father's vegetable garden. The distinctive flower, with its funny point in the middle, was just like the ones on the tomato plants. I knew that the nightshade berries were poison, in spite of the fact that they looked like tiny green tomatoes. I heard there once was a time when people thought the tomato was poisonous; they weren't taking any chances. This type of flower also appears on eggplant, potatoes, and peppers. My powers of observation fell short of instantly recognizing other prominent members of the nightshade family, such as tobacco and petunias, but now that I know, I can see it.

It wasn't until I was checking these spellings that I found that the Latin name for tomato has been changed. Ever since Linnaeus developed his system and started naming everything, people have been disputing names and changing them. It is frustrating for a horticulturist. One uses the Latin name in order to be precise in identification only to find that it's been changed and you have to learn it again. I was amused to find that Carolus Linnaeus himself was later known as Carl von Linné, and not everyone agrees on which name to use.

If you know anything about tomato gardeners you know that this arrangement was made late in the summer. No tomato fancier could possibly cut off the flowers—the future fruits—before she has gotten her fill. By the time I cut these flowers from my 'Sweet 100' I had picked so many fruits that it was no loss. Tomato arrangements look great on a high windowsill, where you can easily see the nodding flowers and the sun illuminates the golden bristles (glandular pubescence) that cover the leaves and stems.

Petroselinum crispum
parsley

Those who know parsley would know from this photo that I grew this parsley last year. It is the flat-leaved kind, which is what I usually grow, but that is not the clue. Parsley is biennial: it blooms only in its second year and then dies. By producing flowers in umbels—clusters of many individual flowers—it makes sure that this one and only chance to reproduce is not wasted. The way plants produce their flowers and how they are attached give clues to who they are and what they want.

Parsley is usually grown as an annual, replaced each year with a young, nonflowering, leafier plant. But planting every *other* year means that I have one more plant to watch as it emerges from dormancy in spring; and, of course, I have the flowers. If picked when the flowers are just opening, the stems will bloom in a vase for a week or two, dropping a cloud of pollen as they go. If you cut after the flowers are gone and seed is formed, the heads are perhaps less delicate but last much longer, with no pollen. They can be dried by hanging them upside down.

Equisetum hymale

horsetails, scouring rush

Is it a coincidence that the Latin name *Equisetum* translates as horse bristles and the plant, which does resemble horsetails, is poisonous to horses? Perhaps its toxicity is related to the fact that its stems contain silica, which gives it its other common name: scouring rush. Equisetum looks as though it would be related to bamboo, but they are subkingdoms apart: bamboo produces flowers and pollen, while equisetum, a truly ancient plant, forms cones and spores as its reproductive method. Regardless of all their other physical similarities, it is this difference between the two that counts to a taxonomist.

Equisetum is, in addition to its spores, famously good at asexual reproduction. It zooms through a garden on underground runners, popping up new plants all along the way, and any bit of a plant that includes a node will root and grow. This makes it an inadvisable addition to one's garden, especially where there is plenty of moisture, which it prefers. Handsome when grown as a container plant (to keep it in check), it is the perfect plant for that pot with no drainage hole, as overwatering is never a problem. Equisetum also makes an excellent cut, which will last in a vase a long, long time. True to form, it roots readily in water and can be potted up and grown on and on.

Schoenoplectus
subtermindis
rush

Rushes live simple lives. Growing in boggy areas, they are not much bothered by competition, disease, or insects. Their blooms, albeit humble, are hermaphroditic; i.e., both sexes are contained in one flower so that they are self-pollinating. This is quite common in the plant world, and such blooms are referred to as "perfect" flowers. It is entertaining to imagine how simple our lives would be if we were "perfect" too.

OPPOSITE
Allium schoenoprasum
chives

Since our Long Island potatoes are not in season at the same time that the chives are coming on strong, and my cooking endeavors in the spring are generally limited, my chives usually do not get cut at the right time for eating, and they go to flower. I am perfectly happy not to come up with more inventive culinary designs on this plant, as I prefer seeing it in bloom. After the flowers are cut the plant will continue to grow. The longevity of the cuts can be prolonged by daily rinsing. Chopping off a bit of the ends helps, too.

Chaenomeles speciosa
common flowering quince

In the language of horticulture, a woody plant that blooms before the leaves emerge is referred to as precocious.

Quince are no longer in favor as a garden plant, but every garden used to have one. The bloom colors can be raucous, the twigs have vicious thorns, and the leaves get mildewed and fall off in the heat of summer. Not much to recommend it but the fact that it forces so well. If you have one and can brave the thorns to get a nice long branch, you are assured success. After two or three months of cold weather, as long as there are some round, plump buds on your stems, stick them in water and they will open. You can get fancy and smash the cut ends, and keep them warmer or colder depending on how quickly you want them to open, but you can hardly

go wrong. You will have the most perfect blossoms, artfully spaced along an eccentrically angled branch. The darker it is in the room where you have them, the paler the blossoms will be. It is a brief moment of bloom, though, and possibly not long enough to justify its parent's surly presence in a space-efficient garden. If it weren't for its flamboyant precociousness lighting up the flower market in winter, the flowering quince could well be lost to cultivation.

In preparation for writing this book I thought I ought to be better informed about how the professionals cut, force, and hold flowering branches. It can get complicated. I read a lengthy timetable for how early each type of branch can be cut, and about keeping the cut branches submerged in vats of cool

water, or in dark rooms at specific temperatures wrapped in plastic, for days and weeks. I knew I would remain an amateur.

My approach to forcing is casual. In late winter when the buds begin to swell, I begin to cut and put the branches in a bucket of warm water. Sometimes, feeling energetic, I smash the stems. The buds are helped along if they are softened with moisture, so I put the bucket in my shower for a day or two and we bathe together. When they start to open I set them out in a spot that's not too bright, and they usually bloom. If I have cut them too early and nothing happens, the branches themselves are nice to have around, and I've done a bit of pruning in the process. I'll try to remember for next year how early is too early.

65

OPPOSITE

Salix x chaenomeloides
ornamental pussy willow

Because they get so large and messy there are almost no appropriate places to plant big weeping willows, but they tempt me. They are one of the first trees to leaf out in the spring, last to drop their leaves in the fall, and many types have bark that glows all winter, intensifying as spring approaches. Fortunately for the timid willow lover, there are the pussy willows. And for the pussy willow lovers, there are the odd, imported varieties that form huge black or rosy silver inflorescences.

I keep mine in the cutting garden because, as great as they look in bloom, I will probably reduce them to the ground by cutting every blooming branch, leaving nothing for the garden. Everyone wants a piece of them. They will grow right back but are not very interesting in summer. I can start cutting for forcing around early February, when the days are getting longer and the buds have begun to swell. Like the colored dogwoods, they root easily in water, so cuttings given to a friend are more than a flower: they are a plant. It works best to get them into soil before they leaf out and use up their stored sugars.

Hamamelis virginiana
witch hazel

Over the winter the supervisor of an arboretum asked if I would like to see his curious witch hazels—two large shrubs, purchased from the same place and planted at the same time. One was leafless, glowing with a heavy bloom; the other had not dropped its dead leaves yet and, although it was blooming just as heavily, the blossoms were hardly visible. He said it would hold the old leaves until the new ones pushed out in spring. It was always the same with these two.

I have noticed the same with witch hazels in the wild when they bloom. Some have leaves; some don't. It's a genetic variation. Because our native witch hazel, virginiana, blooms in the fall, when its leaves, and many others, are the same bright yellow as the blossoms, it is not much noticed. It is worth growing for the cuts because in an arrangement, without competition, the blooms show up well, and you can always cut off some leaves. They smell great, too.

OPPOSITE

Acer platanoides
Norway maple

Environmentalists don't like this tree. It is not native to the United States. Its blossoms are large and plentiful, producing abundant seed that germinates readily. It is disliked because it grows quickly and crowds out less aggressive trees. Brash and prolific, it is short on staying power, as you might expect. The wood is weak and the fall color disappointing, but in bloom it sure is great.

There is a Norway maple in my backyard. It must be self-sown, growing so close to the wall of a former shed that the mower missed it. Its limbs were hanging a bit low, so I waited until late winter to prune them so that I could force the cuts. In a week or so, in a vase, the flowers emerged. In another week or so they began to fade and fall, succeeded by tiny leaves. During three weeks of a late, lingering winter, this thug of the plant world earned its spot in my garden for another year.

Acer rubrum
red maple or swamp maple

Every tree blooms in one way or another. Perhaps the most beautiful flowering tree in the hills of New England is the maple. Then again, oak blossoms are very showy. First the red maples turn a soft rose, followed by the ever-so-chic chartreuse of the sugar maples, and then the Norways, and so on with the oaks. Ever since I realized that the colors of the hills around my home in the spring came from the flowers of the hardwoods, not from their emerging leaves, they have become my favorite flowers of spring. It seems that everyone to whom I point this out is similarly awakened. Once you are aware of them it is hard to believe you never noticed.

The name red maple is a bit misleading. The flowers are red, the twigs are reddish, but the leaves are green—until the fall.

OPPOSITE

Euphorbia cyparissias
cypress spurge

While driving over to a friend's house, I pulled right off a busy road to pick this little spurge. Its remarkable chartreuse was waving at me, even though it is only a few inches tall. As in all euphorbias, the colorful parts are really bracts, not flowers. A well-known example of this is the euphorbia known as poinsettia. Also typical of euphorbias is the sticky white sap. In order to make flowers with sap like this last well in water, you really ought to sear the ends with a flame or boiling water to seal them. Hot tap water works well enough for me. I wonder if my casual attitude would be different if I had paid for these flowers.

Vinca minor
myrtle or periwinkle

When a plant has been brought to new home soil from another country it is referred to as "introduced." Very polite. When that plant finds that it can survive on its own and runs out of the garden into the countryside, it is said to have "escaped from cultivation." Rather menacing. *Vinca minor* is one such plant. Because it is not easy to get a patch started, it has earned the reputation of fragility, but once established it is remarkably tenacious. When I see its demure blanket covering a patch of forest floor I think of it as a Jane of the plant world—pampered child of civilization, escaped to romp in the wild with Tarzan and friends.

This photo was John Hall's idea. I had never thought of using vinca for arranging, a good example of how a thing can be familiar but unseen. Vinca doesn't have much in the way of flower stems, but it more than compensates with its perfect contrast and complement of leaf and flower, not to mention its excellent staying power. It blooms in the spring but the foliage, being evergreen, could be used at any time of the year.

Helianthus annuus
'Velvet Queen' and
'Prado Red'
sunflowers

The old standard 'Mammoth' sunflowers turn their yellow faces to the sun and follow it from east to west, morning to night. If you planted a field of them and your house was on the north side, your army of golden soldiers would all be at attention in the other direction. The new branching-type hybrids are a generation busting loose from such regimentation. They come in many colors and turn any which way.

Sunflowers are in fashion. A large assortment is now available, and last year I grew way too many. I couldn't put them all in my house, or give enough away. Unlike the old-style sunflowers, the new ones will keep producing flowers as long as the old ones are cut. With such abundance, I could indulge myself in cutting the remarkable buds. I even cut the tightest, knowing they wouldn't open.

Sunflowers hold best when cut early in the morning, when the petals are just fully open. An initial dunk in very hot water helps them to last much longer. Immerse them to the neck, then follow that in a bit with immersion in cold water, or simply leave them to cool before arranging.

Barbarea vulgaris
w i n t e r   c r e s s

Jim Cross, the legendary grower, once asked Jim Grimes, an expert on native plants, to give a lecture on soils. This was puzzling to Grimes . . . why me? Because, Cross said, why talk about something you already know? Why not take this opportunity to expand a bit? It is overwhelming how much there is to know in horticulture, and opportunities to take a chance on a new area of understanding are part of the challenge. You just hope, when learning from reading, that you consulted the right author, the one who learned from observation. You hope that your own observations will provide the right foundation for judgment and understanding. Each time your curiosity is challenged an opportunity presents itself to fill in another piece of the puzzle.

I always thought that the puffs of bright yellow in fields in the spring were wild mustard. They are and they aren't. They're winter cress. A member of the same family as mustard (Cruciferae), they tend to grow in moist places, while the later-blooming and similar-looking black mustard (*Brassica nigra*) is usually found in drier fields and waste places. The winter cress, like its cousin water cress, has edible leaves. It is the black mustard that provides the seed for pickling and bird food. An easy way to tell them apart, I have now learned, is that the cress has upright branches while the mustard branches stick out like a scarecrow's arms.

Syringa vulgaris, Viburnum opulus 'Sterile'

common lilac, snowball viburnum

When I was trying to decide whether to buy my house I was having a bout of uncertainty, as it was also a sad time in my life. I stopped by one spring day to look at it again and there, right outside the bedroom window, one of the biggest *Viburnum opulus* 'Sterile' I had ever seen (it is the one that is the best for cuts—the one I always wanted), lost in the midst of a tangle of overgrown foundation plants and just about to bloom. It needed a lot of pruning, so there were plenty of branches for guilt-free cutting. Of course I am happy living here—my life with plants has been nothing but happy—so why not read them as good omens?

Lilacs are the perfect shrubs for cutting. In my childhood, one of our few neighbors on a country dirt road was a family that lived in a dilapidated farmhouse with a magnificent lilac bush. Because they could use the money, each year when it came into bloom they would cut all the flowers off and sell them. As usual with lilacs, by midsummer it looked mildewed and scruffy, but the following spring it would always produce the most amazing quantity of blossoms. I have decided that thorough flower removal (i.e., dead-heading) was the reason. I have recently planted a selection of lilacs in my cutting garden. They are in the back, where I won't see much of them, and when they bloom I plan to cut every last blossom. Perhaps, if things get tough, I'll have a source of supplemental income.

When you cut viburnums and lilacs they will last longer if you cut as much stem as your shrub can spare, re-cut and smash the ends, and remove all or most of the leaves when arranging. To keep the shrub itself feeling young, occasionally cut some of the biggest, oldest branches right to the ground in the spring. Cut out inward-growing branches, too, to keep plenty of light and air available throughout. Make all your cuts just above a node. Don't worry too much. One of the characteristics of the perfect shrub for cutting is a great capacity for forgiving.

Naturally, clover is overlooked as a good cut flower. It is everywhere. It doesn't require any special attention. It doesn't command much, either, until you get close. The blossoms are actually rotund bundles of tightly furled flowers. The leaves of red clover, ordinarily in threes, can be distinguished from those of other clovers by the sophisticated silver chevron on each one. An interesting contrast to its simple country message.

OPPOSITE

Rumex acetosella
common sorrel or sheep sorrel

Human beings might as well be grouped by their preferences, as plants are. The subspecies to which I belong could be loosely divided into two varieties: "plant (flora) people" and "animal (fauna) people." Although I have an inordinate affection for my cat, I am not curious about her lineage. I don't even know her Latin name. With plants it is different. I can hardly wait to get to know the name of every new one I come across.

One year for Father's Day our Brownie project was to make a bookmark by pressing something we liked between two pieces of exposed (clear) movie film and stitching them together with yarn through the sprocket holes. I chose a bit of wildflower and thought it one of the most beautiful things ever made by Brownie hands. Now I know its name is *Rumex*, and that it provides nourishment for a number of small and large animals as well as for my imagination.

Sheep sorrel can be found growing in large stands in dry, sandy, acid soils in full sun. A single plant would be barely noticeable, but as it spreads readily by seed and root in areas with little competition it is easy to spot and is beautiful. The flowers range from green to red, and male and female flowers are on separate plants.

Trifolium pratense, Poa pratensis
red clover, Kentucky bluegrass

This picture could recall an American country childhood, even for those who didn't have one. I might also have included dandelions, except their stems get mushy so quickly they are no good for cutting. None of these plants is American, though. Not strictly speaking, anyway. They were brought from Europe, both wittingly and un-. They have been here so long, and are so ubiquitous, they are part of our verbal and visual lore. There are crusaders in the world of horticulture who would like to restrict the use of non-native plants, even eradicate them in some cases. That seems a bit simplistic. Perhaps we are taking too much credit for our role as vectors and too little responsibility for our role as thinkers and caregivers.

Hydrangea paniculata
'Grandiflora'
P.G. (Peegee) hydrangea

The study of how people interact with plants is called ethnobotany. In addition to our active interactions, such as the culinary and herbal, there are passive ones, like nostalgia. Images of flowers, branches, and leaves all evoke strong memories and inspire passion—personal, familial, nationalistic.

There must have been a moment around fifty years ago when it was imperative to plant Peegees in every cemetery. Plants as fashion. They are now fully grown and have assumed the vase shape of the mature plant. They are in fashion again. When I am looking for a big old one with the characteristic shape to buy for a client, I ask for a "cemetery Peegee" and the suppliers know what I mean.

In order to get Peegees to dry well without wilting, do not pick them until they are fully open and the pinkish color is showing. Later is also okay. I like to put them in a smallish amount of water and just let the water dry up. Large quantities can be hung upside down in a dry, dark place.

OPPOSITE

Baccharis halimifolia
groundsel tree

Many years ago, while trying to restore some beauty to a disturbed and bereft piece of sandy land adjacent to salt water, I noticed a number of plants that had apparently seeded in and looked healthy. They had attractive leaves and tended to be somewhat shrublike. No one knew what they were other than "weeds." When they bloomed at the end of summer I was impressed again. This time I found out what the plant was but was warned to stay away from it as a "nasty, invasive weed." So I left it alone. Nevertheless, I continued to admire it as a plant that liked difficult situations. My favorite stand thrives along the highway that passes through the massive New York City dump on Staten Island. Each fall, on my way to buy trees in New Jersey, I have seen them in bloom and thought, Hmmm . . . I don't see them taking over any valuable property. Two years ago one appeared in a neglected, difficult part of a client's flower border. I asked the weeder to leave it. It is now a handsome plant, and shows no signs yet of bad behavior. Oddly, it was named for the god Bacchus, renowned for bad behavior, but no one seems to know the real story.

Lately, I have noticed others taking note of this plant. It is making a big fall showing in the flower market. There is very little else that time of year that is blooming on a branch. Actually, it isn't flower petals you notice at all. First you see the pappi, little bristles arranged around the insignificant bloom. These are followed by the tiny fruits, each with a showy tuft of white hairs.

If groundsel is cut after the flowers are formed, they will continue in their development and go on to form the ornamental fluffy fruits. I expected these to fly all around and make a big mess if I tried to keep them too long, but they didn't; they held on and on. Not bad for a weed from the dump.

Cirsium vulgare
bull thistle

The image of the thistle has been made into a national symbol. Just as the lily was stylized as the French fleur de lis, the thistle was adopted and adapted by the Scots. Its peculiar architecture, making it easily recognizable, is surely a factor, as is its ability to survive.

Since the common thistle is a legendary survivor, invasive in the garden and a bane to hay farmers, why doesn't it take over? Maybe it is because it fends off help as well as predators. Just about impossible to handle, it has thorns that pierce the thickest gloves, so that in spite of its beauty it is unwelcome in meadow or garden. I find this perverse contrariness alluring and like to compare arranging bull thistles to lion taming.

Rosa 'Dainty Bess'

All the members of the family Rosaceae have five sepals. They are the five green points of the star at the base of an apple or the five green "fingers" that clasp a rose bud. If you pick a rose before the sepals begin to curl away from the bud, it will never open. Sometimes I like to pick them too early on purpose so they remain as buds—eternal youth.

There are so many variables that determine how well a cut rose will last that you could make an endless study—type of rose, stage of development, time of day, time of year, weather conditions, length of stem, leaves left on or removed, direction of cut (knife or pruners?), temperature of water, depth of water, water additives, temperature of room, amount of sunlight, opacity of vase, and so on. This is only one small aspect of rose culture, and roses are only one (albeit numerous) type of cut flower. This could leave you feeling exhausted, frightened, or addicted.

I can't live long enough to experiment with all the variables so I apply logic as a poultice to my madness. Longevity in a vase can be directly related to how much energy the flower still needs to bloom versus how much sustenance has been provided. The more sugar reserves it carries with it, and the more water it can take up, the longer it will last. A flower picked young is going to need a lot of energy. Picked too young, it will need too much. I figure that whatever I can do to assist these needs—like picking when the transpiration rate is low and turgidity high (early in the day), taking plenty of stem, cutting to expose maximum uptake surface to water (at a slant), keeping transpiration rate low (away from heat and sunlight)—will most likely be best. It is working.

Zinnia elegans 'Whirligig'

Our notions of beauty are often applied to, as much as derived from, the plant world. Controlled hybridization has given breeders this power. Bigger, bolder, brighter. When fashion dictates, a flower is developed, sure to please. Plants are generally very obliging in this way.

Hybridizers have had many "successes," but one of their big goals seems to have eluded them: a pure white marigold. A major seed company offered a reward to any person who grew one and handed it over for propagation. Apparently someone won, as I haven't seen the offer lately, but where is the white marigold? Not really white enough yet, perhaps; or maybe a marigold just doesn't look good in white, although I can hardly imagine that would concern them. It hasn't kept white zinnias (which always look dull and dirty) off the market. Odd that people are fixed on white in a flower that doesn't have much going for it other than its intense colors. Black is another sought-after color, as well as true blue. Not because they are necessarily going to complement a flower's form but because it just has to be narcotic to have the power to create a new living thing. Who knows what is too much?

I ordered the seed for this zinnia by mistaking its name for that of a far more modest one. When I saw the photo on the pack I thought the flowers looked frightening, but of course I couldn't throw the seed away. Although discordant in my garden, they become little marvels in a vase by themselves. The colors and markings play up the arrangement of the petals in a happy way. As fashion and markets and hybrids go, I doubt it will be long before this child of science is abandoned for an "improved" form, and, being most likely sterile, it may disappear altogether, a victim of a speeded-up version of survival of the fittest—with questionable aesthetics as criteria. But strength alone (a human's notion of strength) has never altogether defined the fittest.

possibly *Triadenum virginicum*

I stuck this little flower in my wildflower field guide one day while out poking around. I couldn't find it listed so I saved it to identify at another time, using another reference book. I often come across it, still unnamed, and delight in the way it waits for me, pretty much the way it was when I first collected it.

It gives me pause to think about how happily plants succumb to my will, how they often look good when treated badly. I have never thought to save one of those frogs I find flattened and dried on a dirt road after a summer of being run over. It is such a different thing. Is it because I am an animal and not a plant or because plants don't bleed?

Polygonum cuspidatum
Japanese knotweed or
Mexican bamboo

When Frederick Law Olmsted was building
Central Park in New York City, he imported
plants from far and wide. Legend has it that
this was one of them. One he thought would
be tough enough to take difficult urban
park conditions yet interesting enough to
provide ornamental value. Its toughness
way outstripped its ornament, and when it
began to move into and take over all its
neighboring plantings, drastic measures
were employed to remove it. Naturally they
couldn't get it all, and, being tough and
smart, it headed straight out of town, where
it would not be bothered. It remains, ornamental on rural roadsides and a tough adver-
sary in domestic landscapes. Perhaps it was
ahead of its time and in the wrong park; there
are plenty of urban spaces now that could
use something—anything.

Rhus glabra
smooth sumac

Sumac is one of my personal, private plants.
As common as it is on country roadsides, and
despite its uncommon beauty, it goes largely
unnoticed. I think it is a "four-season" plant,
providing interest all year: the young foliage,
delicate and ferny in the spring; the fashion-
able green flowers in summer; a great fall display of leaves and seed heads; and in winter
a curious, skeletonlike framework that casts
forked shadows on the snow. Easy to grow,
it seldom is used in the cultivated landscape.
I am planning to plant a grove in my little
backyard meadow, where it will grow like a
tiny forest. It is stoloniferous (spreads by
underground runners), and when it gets too
thick I will have extras to cut. The birds will
love it, and so will my friends when they sit
within its personal, private space.

Hibiscus syriacus
rose of Sharon

OPPOSITE
Antirrhinum majus
snapdragons

What if we used the same words to describe the reproductive parts of plants as we use for our own genitalia? Would it make us less enamored of flowers, or less ashamed of ourselves? Every flower's timing, color, and form have a purpose—to attract a pollinator who will move the pollen from a male part (stamen) to a female part (pistil). It is seductive to contemplate. Hibiscus and snapdragons use opposite techniques of attraction, one practically throwing it at you and the other keeping its prize hidden, allowing only those who alight on its pendulous lips into its embrace.

A short, random, overgrown hedge of old rose of Sharons was growing on my property when I moved in, and I will keep it. They are such undemanding plants to grow and cut. They hardly need pruning, but there is always plenty to cut without harming their shape. They last well, the spent flowers replaced by those that were not quite open when I brought them in. The snapdragons did not come from my garden, though. Only florists or more diligent gardeners than I can grow the long, long stems that are best for arranging. If you don't keep cutting them, they stop blooming, and the long ones need staking to keep from flopping in the mud.

Lilium 'Casablanca'
Casablanca lily

These days scientists are finding out more and more about a plant's sex life. Once a flower has been pollinated, it sends the petals a message to drop off—it doesn't need that catch-me-love-me look any more. Its life, however, is hardly over. It is still beautiful and you can tell more about its lineage when it is undressed. Sometimes you can watch the ovary swell as it begins the process of forming seeds. While still attached to its plant, it continues making the seeds and sends a message to the rest of the plant to stop blooming, to save energy: reproduction complete—resume vegetative growth. It follows, therefore, that if a flower can be prevented from pollinating it will last longer.

This is why the stamens are removed from lilies when you get them from a good florist. In addition, if the flowers are removed before setting seed, the plant will be stronger and may continue to bloom.

I bought these lilies in the flower market because it was winter when I decided I wanted to include them in this book. I rummaged around to find some with the stamens still on and handed them over to be wrapped. The well-trained clerk immediately yanked off the anthers—the pollen heads. I had to find another batch, open enough to see the pollen but not starting to fall apart. She then showed me how, if I rolled a ripe bud gently between my palms, it would open at my touch.

Clematis lanuginosa 'Candida',

O P P O S I T E
Clematis montana

Clematis has two personalities. Its flowering persona, the better known, has made it a popular vine in gardens of all persuasions. A strong floral display combined with a usually weak stem and leaf apparatus make it ideal for climbing on things (like other plants) without overwhelming them. After the blooms fade it becomes its other, less recognized self: a subtle explosion of seed heads with wildly elongated and waving styles. Clematis blossoms vary considerably in color, size, and shape. The seed heads vary mostly in size and prominence—not necessarily related to those of their petaled precedents. They last well into the winter, the larger and more numerous ones looking much like a legion of Valley girls tossing their hair.

Pollen

Symplocarpus foetidus
skunk cabbage

I am one of the lucky people who had a country childhood. Down the (dirt) road from our house lived an old lady who knew all kinds of neat stuff. She lived without electricity or running water in a house filled with amazing collections of natural and crafted objects. She had a dried, inflated blowfish hanging from the ceiling. She told me that skunk cabbages can grow so early in the spring, right through ice, because they generate heat. I have since read that the heat is a result of their extraordinary rate of metabolism. They do grow awfully fast; it is easy to miss the flowers if you are not waiting and watching for them. It wasn't until I grew up to be a plant person that I thought about what they are and how they work. Every plant's flowers need to be pollinated—by wind or insect. With their hoods pulled over their heads, skunk cabbage blooms can hardly make their pollen available to the wind. Insects? In the winter? What about that smell? Flies. On warmish late-winter days, dazed and hungry flies come out of dormancy and, following their preference for things foetid, become the skunk cabbages' consorts.

My attraction to skunk cabbage blooms may raise unflattering questions, but every year I just have to find some and bring them home. They don't last terribly well, unless you have a very cool house. And the smell . . . it doesn't persist, or perhaps it's that I like it.

Ambrosia artemisiifolia
ragweed

Solidago rugosa
rough-stemmed goldenrod

I spend a bit of time each summer in defense of goldenrod. It has such a bad reputation for spreading misery—allergies—but the fact is that goldenrod is guilty of nothing more than showing off. It calls attention to itself with its bright, ubiquitous blooms at the same time that ragweed, the aptly named real culprit, is in bloom. This can be confirmed with a sort of logic. Goldenrod, with its flashy display, has attracted and is buzzing with bees, on whom it depends for pollination. The plain, green-flowered ragweed stands alone, no bees, its pollen all carried on the wind. Aha! Unless a bee flew up your nose, you would be unlikely to get a dose of goldenrod pollen.

Goldenrod makes a great addition to arrangements, picked when the blossoms are just opening. With all its leaves stripped off, it looks so good and holds so well that it is hard to believe its bad rap perseveres. In ancient times, when it seems people had more natural sense, it was regarded for its healing powers. Ragweed, on the other hand, has very little but oddity to recommend it. Or perhaps it offers a nifty way to relocate unwanted guests.

Betula pendula
white birch

It is unlikely that birch would ever be named
as a popular plant to cut for flowers, but very
little escapes my pruners. In the spring, when
the flowers (catkins) are formed, there are
males and females. The pollen, produced by
the males, is distributed as much by gravity as
by wind. On calm days it rains down, enough
to leave a coat of yellow dust on anything
below, like your car. The parts pictured here
are really not the flowers but the cones that
the female flowers have become. Each is a
tidy stack of flat little seeds that will break
apart in rough winter weather and scatter on
the ground. In the less active air of my home
they just hang on, pretty much until I get
tired of them and go cut up something else
to scrutinize and admire.

Rosa multiflora, Rosa sevillana, Rosa rugosa

There is a famous saying that there is no history, just biography. The history of the rose has been written into the biographies of people and populations: the Empress Josephine, so nuts about roses that she underwrote the considerable cost of Redouté's rose portraits; the War of the Roses; the children of England, suffering from their impoverished diet during World War II, saved from scurvy by the rediscovery of an ancient remedy—the vitamin C in rose hips. The history of the rose has also been written as the biography of the roses themselves. How the tea rose came from China with the tea trade and was introduced to the European Damask and Gallica roses. How

they were married and produced and married and produced some more. How they came to be what they are today, intermingled with the lives of those who have bred them for new roses and those who have carefully maintained the old stock so that it would not be lost. How their names, in the midst of countless offspring, and plenty of bickering, have been preserved. A rose by any other name?

Most of the old roses bloom just once a year. Most of the newer ones have been bred to keep producing flowers throughout the summer. If the faded blooms are not cut off they will go to seed in the form of small red fruits called hips, and further blooms will be inhibited. Because the hips are often highly

decorative, the last roses of the season can be left on, and as the weather cools the color of the hips will get stronger. Some roses make more and better hips than others. There are some that are grown for the hips more than for the flowers—they provide color, and cuts, and bird food in the winter garden.

I will always have plenty of the *multiflora* rose to cut all throughout any winter. It grows wild in a massive tangle along my back property line, home to flocks of birds who are safe and well fed in there. I have an arrangement of the hips by my bed, which I cut at least a month or so ago. It has long since run out of water and would look as good as new but for the dust.

Berberis thunbergii
Japanese barberry

The barberries are an example of a plant genus that gets its reputation and common name from its prominent thorns and fruit. There is another, more intimate attribute that the barberries share: if you break or cut into a stem or root, the interior is a vivid yellow. Following my usual practice of trying to think of a logical reason for everything in nature, I have decided that the thorns protect the berries from grazing animals and save them for the birds, who will swallow them whole, digest only the flesh, and deposit the seed, along with its own little manure pile, to thrive in another locale. In the farm fields of New England grazed by dairy cattle, the only vegetation that remains is the clusters of *Berberis vulgaris*. A form introduced from Europe, it is unpopular with farmers but has made itself an ornamental bird haven in areas otherwise grazed to a monotonous monoculture. I haven't any ideas about the yellow innards, though.

Pyracantha 'Navajo'
firethorn

As a member of the rose family, pyracantha might be expected to have a rose's characteristic strengths and weaknesses: it has lovely, albeit small, flowers, great berries (the same as a rose's hips), and is susceptible to fungus diseases. The thorns are a particular strength. Extremely well developed and sharp, they also have more than the usual share of the "poison" that makes a rose thorn's puncture wound especially painful, often aching for days (the natural opener for many fairy tales). The Royal Hort says that the fire in firethorn refers to the color of the berries, but common knowledge as I interpret it says it's the thorns.

Malus
crab apple

Fruit that remains on a plant long after the leaves have dropped is referred to in horticulture as persistent. I like the directness of that. It is a habit that is generally, maybe always, considered desirable. Not all varieties of the same plant will have the same amount of persistence, as with apples. Some start falling off the moment they are ripe. Bruised and rotting and abuzz with yellow jackets, they provide an uninvited mulch that is probably good for the tree but marginally ornamental. Some apples hold on well into the winter, getting smaller and darker and wizened but remaining consistently attractive and available as food for cold-weather foragers.

There is an empty lot across the street from my house that, judging by the size of the trees, was mowed until about eight or ten years ago. There are a number of crab apples mixed in with cedars and bayberries and wild rose. Because they are from seed of mixed parentage, the crabs naturally vary quite a bit. The variations are especially apparent in their progeny, the apples, in terms of size, color (red to yellow), and persistence. I think I have located the parent(s) of this family of colorful individuals in the backyard of a neighboring house.

I cut the branch for this picture from the largest of the wildlings. Growing just at the edge of the mowed road shoulder, it has prospered. I am cutting only the branches that will improve its shape in the hopes that, should this lot get cleared again, it will be spared.

Because the branches of a tree do not use much water in the winter, they can exist quite nicely without any. I like arranging without a vase because that way a branch can be presented horizontally, the way it grew.

Cucurbita pepo
" w e d d i n g   g o u r d "

Last year I bought and planted some gourd seeds sold as "Choose Your Weapon Mix." I was expecting the big gourds: the dipper and bird house and bowl gourds. What I got were mostly the ubiquitous, boring little striped and warty gourds sold everywhere at Halloween and Thanksgiving, plus the one that kept me from being terribly disappointed: a small white gourd with a luminous pale green glow. I brought it to a wedding luncheon to contribute to the decor and named it the wedding gourd.

This year I definitely have the right seeds for the big gourds, plus some new information. The little ones have yellow flowers like squash; the big ones have white flowers. Both are domesticated; they have lost their ability to survive in the wild, but for reasons of use and ornament rather than food they have been preserved.

magic powers. I fed them to my dolls. I squashed the juice out of them and used it to stain my nails purple.

Ethnobotanists believe that children may retain traces of ancient human/plant relationships. It interests me to think that my childhood games may have been rooted in long lost rituals of adornment and survival.

Two things I have learned about poke as an adult: when they are young the leaves are not poisonous and are very tasty; the plant, when cut, lasts an incredibly long time in water.

OPPOSITE

Rubus odoratus
purple-flowering raspberry

As more and more people have less and less direct contact with nature, we are becoming understandably more insecure about eating anything found out there. Most of us seem to still feel safe with members of the genus *Rubus*, perhaps because they are also culti-vated and sold in little containers we all recognize. There are dozens of different members of the *Rubus* clan, all quite similar and sometimes difficult to identify. When you pick and eat the berries yourself it becomes easier to recognize their differences. Some are sweet, some are killer sour. Some are especially thorny. When ripe, blackberries come off their stems whole, with a solid cen-ter. The ones called black caps or black rasp-berries come off hollow, leaving a little white cone behind. They taste the best, and the birds usually get them first.

Phytolacca americana
pokeweed

As country kids, my brothers and sisters and I knew that there were a few easily recognized berries that were okay to eat, and all the rest were best left alone. A berry I always "knew" to be poisonous was pokeberry. I don't recall being taught this, but we kids all knew it. Nevertheless, or perhaps because of this, I developed an interest in them. I gave them

OPPOSITE

Cynara scolymus
artichoke

As a food plant the artichoke doesn't appear any more palatable than the other thistles in its family. Most thistles have used their considerable defenses to great advantage and have spread themselves around the world. Artichokes have gone the other way, and do not appear outside of cultivation. This means that should a field of them be left to fend for itself it would be lacking an essential defense: the ability to successfully compete. Its looks are certainly deceiving.

Ligustrum ovalifolium
California privet

Many birds depend on berries. They need them for nourishment all winter long, when there's not much else. There are some kinds of berries that get instantly devoured in the fall and other kinds that are left for later. Is this a remarkable display of discipline on the part of the birds? Not really—they get a lot of help from the berries. Some berries need to freeze and thaw and ferment a bit before they taste good to birds. Nature's preserves for birds.

During the summer the privet berries are green and, although abundant, are not noticeable within the foliage. Then the first frost hits the leaves and the berries begin to color, going completely black within a few frosty nights.

I think because they are black, and perhaps because they are so common where I live, no one notices the beauty of privet berries. This adds to their impact when people see them in a vase and realize what they are. Since privet *always* needs pruning, I hack away at it with glee. It makes a good cut. The berries don't fall off and make a mess.

You have got to be poised to pounce if you want to cut some with berries. As soon as they begin to ripen, the birds devour them. I like them when they are turning from green to black, just when the nights get cold, just before the birds want them.

OPPOSITE BOTTOM

Maclura pomifera
Osage orange

Although I have found no documented evidence of arrowwood having really been used for arrows, *Maclura*, whose other common name is bow wood, really was used for bows, and apparently still is. The wood, highly rot-resistant, was also used for fence posts. In the early West, the thorny trees were planted as living fencerows. The wood contains about one percent 2,3,4,5-tetrahydroxystilbene, which does not sound like a naturally occurring substance, but it is. It does sound toxic, which it is—to a number of fungi. This may or may not be related to the fact that the fruit makes an effective roach repellent, and the milky sap causes contact dermatitis in certain people. What connection these people might have with fungi and roaches has not, to my knowledge, been researched.

The fruit, for which the tree is now best known, is inedible and defies comparison. It certainly is not much like an orange other than being round. Michael Dirr, Professor (aka hero) of Horticulture at the University of Georgia, who has a way with words, describes it as a "four-to-six-inch wide globose syncarp of drupes covered with a mamillate ring, yellow-green in color." As children we called them road apples. We liked to put them out in the road and wait for cars to drive over them. They have an exciting, mysterious quality, and perhaps we thought something toxic would happen.

Cornus racemosa
gray dogwood

The shining white berries of gray dogwood have limited ornamental value in the landscape. They are the kind that gets eaten immediately. If you get to them before the birds, they are ornamental in a vase. The leaves may drop off quickly, but the berries and their bright red pedicels (stems) remain. In the wild, with the berries gone, the pedicels become the ornament.

OPPOSITE TOP

Viburnum dentatum
arrowwood

This shrub is a common edge-of-woods plant in much of the eastern United States, and it adapts well to gardens. Like other viburnums, its leaves are opposite, but unlike others, it has stiffly straight, narrow stems. This gives rise to its common name. I have been told that the Indians used it to make arrows but believe this to be a romantic concept.

Ilex verticillata
winterberry holly

Most people think of hollies as evergreens with bright red berries at Christmas. Not all hollies have red berries, and not all are evergreen. Hollies are all dioecious, however, which means that there are separate male and female plants. Only the females have the berries—this is critical to remember when purchasing a holly, if berries are the object. Of course, a totally female population is not going to produce any fruit, so there's got to be a male somewhere in the neighborhood.

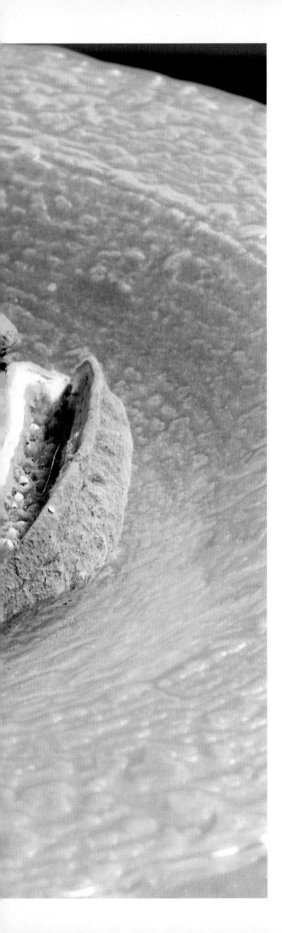

seed collection

A seed is an embryo looking for a good home. Its parent plant has invariably found some remarkable way of packaging it to send it out on its quest, suitably dressed for the journey to the kind of spot in which its type tends to prosper. They fall straight down at the feet of their parents like the proverbial apple, fly off on the wind, cling to a shaggy coat for the ride, get eaten and deposited elsewhere, float down a stream—endless invention and variation.

seed pods (assorted)

When I travel, I keep an eye out for interesting seed pods to bring home as mementos. I seldom remember which ones I got where, but all together they make a pleasing and mysterious collective travel memory. Once I came home to find my home full of fluff—a pod had burst and ejected its seeds.

That one had traveled to the wrong place on the wrong criterion—its good looks.

Lilium 'Casablanca'
Casablanca lily

It would be hard to convince me that looks have nothing to do with how a plant prospers. Otherwise, why would they be so faultlessly beautiful, young and old, inside and out, alive and dead?

Lilies are so prized as a cut flower that they usually don't stay in a cutting garden long enough to go to seed. Any bloom not cut for arrangements is usually removed when it fades to prevent it from going to seed and sapping energy from the plant for next year's blooms. I like the seed pods well enough not to be terribly concerned about next year's blossom count. They last all winter in a dry vase.

OPPOSITE
Acer platanoides
Norway maple

I like to imagine that the template for everything we will ever invent already exists in seed pods. The samaras, as the winged pods of maples are called, make little helicopters when dropped from a height, and if you break one in half at the joint, then carefully split the seed pod open and place it on the end of your nose, it will stick there very nicely.

Ipomoea alba
moonflower

The moonflower, opening as the sun sets, is like the morning glory's yang. Blooming at night, glowing pure white, with an incredible perfume, it is obviously looking for a different sort of suitor than its perky daytime cousin. Who is there to pollinate it at night? Usually it is moths but the fact that its seed heads are huge and strange and dark purple (as compared to the much more normal-looking morning glory progeny) raises questions about the relationship between plant and pollinator; these are rather bat-like.

Tulipa 'Spring Green'
tulip

If you don't cut tulips when the buds are tight they will fall apart quickly in a vase. The fallen petals are messy, but in falling they reveal the beautiful pods within. If you leave tulips in the garden until the petals fall, the mess is missed and the pods, having had more time to develop, are far more impressive and long-lasting. It is a pleasant justification for not having picked them earlier.

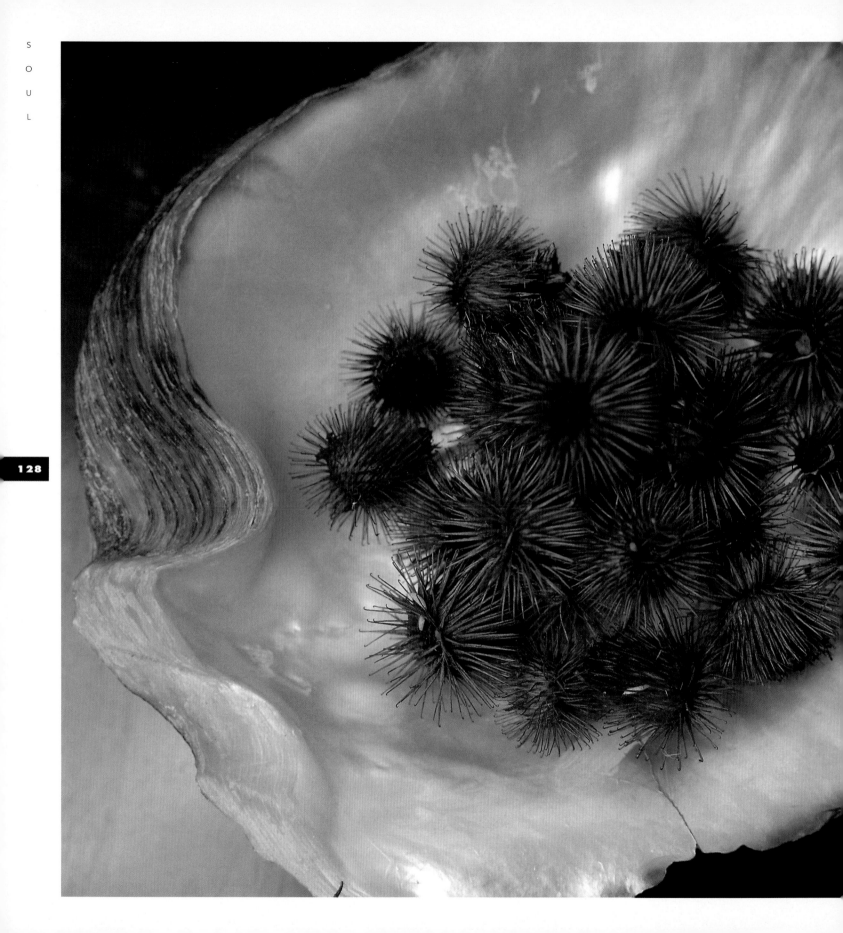

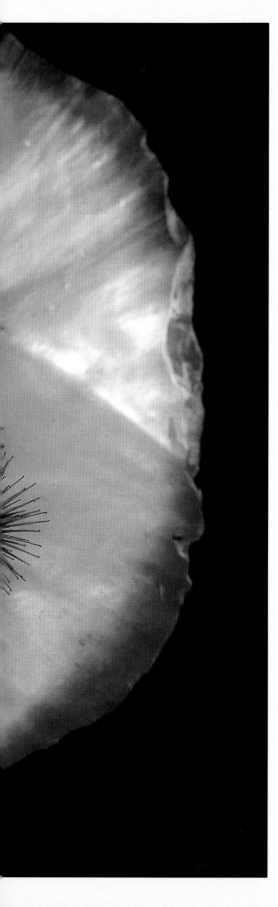

Arctium minus

common burdock

I have heard that Velcro was invented by
a shepherd inspired by burrs on his sheep.
I like this myth for its romantic blend of
past and future. Surely he lived happily
ever after, being well rewarded for his
acute observation.

Physalis alkekengi
Chinese lantern

The fruit of this *Physalis*, like those of many other members of the nightshade family (Solanaceae), is said to be somewhat poisonous before it fully ripens. This one, the ornamental one, protects its unripe fruit with a bright orange capsule. It can be picked at this time and hung to dry. If left in the garden, the flesh of the capsule will melt, leaving just its skeleton and its visible, now edible, so tempting fruit with ready-for-distribution seeds inside.

Arisaema triphyllum
jack-in-the-pulpit

Poking around in the woods reminds me acutely of my childhood, when I had endless choices of how to fill the time while waiting to grow up. Often I would head outside with no particular goal but to be there, and something always turned up.

Jack-in-the-pulpits had a mystical quality then, and I would (and still do) carefully step around them and never, never pick one. I found these seeds lying on a bed of leaves while I was peeking under a shrub. It made me feel like I had found a bird's egg, but I know that if I put them back in the woods they will not have been doomed by their brief foray into the world of home decor.

Rumex crispus, Amaranthus retroflexus, Vaccinium corymbosum
sour dock highbush, pigweed, highbush blueberry

There are two sorts of plants in this picture, with two personas.

The weeds are doing well in housing starts. When a construction project keeps the soil disturbed, trampled, and compacted for a year or so, there is very little that survives. Dock and pigweed are among the only inhabitants, growing from the hard-packed soil in spots where they won't get mauled. Unwelcome in any managed landscape, farm or home, they seem to be very happy under such adverse conditions and, until I came along, would have gone unnoticed and left untouched. The blueberry, on the other hand, hates change. Difficult to grow and highly prized, it is found in places long left alone. I like an arrangement with subtext.

Asclepias syriaca
m i l k w e e d

The critical part that milkweed plays in a monarch butterfly's life cycle has brought favorable attention to a previously un-appreciated weed. The glycosides in its honey (a staple of the butterfly's diet), which make monarchs taste too disgusting for predators to eat, also affect the milky sap. Cows, who are not fussy, must know this and eat around milkweed, leaving it to go to seed and ruin a field for grazing or hay. Farmers then do their best to eradicate it. Recently, a human use for the floss has been found: as a hypoallergenic alternative to goose down for pillows. Ironically, attempts to cultivate milkweed have been unsuccessful, as it becomes disease-prone when grown in quantity as a monoculture.

Milkweed blossoms occur in bunches, called cymes, containing about twenty or so flowers apiece. Only one flower in each cyme will develop a seed capsule. Would that be the first one to be pollinated, like sperm and eggs?

Castanea mollissima
Chinese chestnut

OPPOSITE
Liquidambar styraciflua
American sweet gum

Successful pods protect their seeds with some wonderfully wicked enclosures, but in today's tidy world these defenses may ultimately sabotage their parents' survival.

The need for the chestnut's food and the sweet gum's aromatic balsam has become obsolete, making these trees solely dependent on their ornamental value to remain in the horticultural trade. Their visual attributes are seriously undermined by their exuberant, defiant production of pods that litter the ground with spiny and prickly remains from fall to late winter.

The sweet gum has a shiny, uniform shape and such glorious fall color that it can be enjoyed from a distance. It is holding its own, offered by most nurseries in many named varieties. One of the Chinese chestnut's commanding qualities is its size, so very few people have the space anymore for its novelty. It is not a native American tree like the sweet gum. For all the imports that have made themselves at home here there are probably just as many who did not get to stay.

CLOCKWISE
FROM UPPER RIGHT
*Ipomoea alba, Phaseolus sp,
Dolichos lablab, Cucurbita
pepo, Tropaeolum majus*
moonflower, pole beans,
hyacinth bean, gourd,
assorted nasturtiums

It is one of my favorite casual miracles that
the seeds I save from my plants, or get in the
mail, contain life. There was recently a much-
reported story about a scientist in California
who managed to germinate one lotus seed
from among a group of seven found in a dry
lake bed in China. It was carbon tested and
found to be 1,288 years old. "The seed must
have a really good system of handling stress,"
said the scientist.

Basics of Flower Arranging

People look wistfully at my house filled with its usual odd assortment of branches and seeds and buds and suggest that I have some special knack. Not so, just a passion; and lots of practice. So, as an addendum to this book full of passion, these are some thoughts on practicing.

SIMPLICITY

The easiest way to succeed in this is to use one flower, one bud, one leaf. Or, a few of the same thing. Remember that the object is to bring attention to a particular aspect of beauty or interest: color or shape or texture. Quantity is not necessary, or even advantageous.

CROWDING

Allow for space and air. Very few flowers can look good when they are crammed in together, and even if they do, you lose their individual beauty. Remove most of the leaves; you need far fewer than you might think. You can always cut some separately and add them back in strategic locations. Always remove everything from the stem below the waterline to prevent rotting. Cutting all thorns and branch nubs off makes it easier to position stems, as they don't get caught on one another.

COMPLEMENTS AND CONTRASTS

An arrangement's relationship to its container and its space is essential. The shape and size of a vase should be complementary to and consistent with what is in it. The same goes for where you place it. An open spot in a big room calls for a large arrangement, an intimate spot on a small table for the opposite. The size and texture of the plant material should follow: Delicate arrangements are best in a spot where you will be close and still, coarse textures and bold shapes will catch your eye as you pass by. Place intricate patterns in front of simple backgrounds and vice versa. Put bright colored flowers in simple, dark colored vases for a formal room and in contrasting, bright colored vases for a less serious space. Do the same with textures. Be playful with the message, like putting a common weed in a fancy vase. When you use clear vases, the stems become part of the arrangement, so don't ignore them. The water, too, is an element; make sure it is clean and consider experimenting with the level. In the end, what makes a good arrangement is not so much any special talent but the practice of taking *everything* into consideration. This is why prearranged purchased flowers tend to look professional, not personal.

LIGHTING

Think about the light source for where the arrangement will be placed. Grasses and diaphanous petals look radiant when backlit. Dark colors benefit from a lamp nearby. There are no arrangements that like direct sunlight.

STAND BACK

While you are making your arrangement, keep stepping back and checking it from different distances. If you have the room, walk around your work. Otherwise, just keep turning it, or plan on placing it where it will be visible from only one side.

ACCESSORIES

A few flower-arranging supplies can come in handy to get things to stay in place. Frogs, especially pin frogs, the weighted discs that look like a little bed of nails, are my favorites. They come in all sizes to fit into most vases and hold stems up so you can get more space and individuality. Though they are weighted to stay upright, heavy branches will tip them over, in which case you can add some florist's clay, which will help stick the base flat in the container. Additionally, there are frogs that have a sort of basketlike grid for additional support higher up on the stems. Some pin frogs even come as part of a metal dish (page 105) and are great for tiny little things such as species narcissus. You can't make a bad arrangement with them as long as you don't overcrowd it. There are wonderful frogs to be found in antique stores. Most of them are more ornamental than useful, meant for glass vases or wide shallow dishes where you will be able to see them, but they are fun to collect. Traditional and professional flower arrangers often use a product called Oasis. This is a block of green foam, which you put into the bottom of a container and then you poke stems into. The holes don't fill back in when you pull the stems out, so it does not work for repeat arrangements.

My favorite scissors for arranging are the Joyce Chen rubber-handled scissors sold for the kitchen. For heavy stems and in the garden, I use Felco #2 pruners.

For cleaning stubborn stains out of small-mouthed vases, try a foaming denture cleaner.

There are many more accessories and techniques available to explore for those who wish to enter into the more formalized world of flower arranging. The Garden Club of America has classes and competitions. Many cities have ikebana clubs. There are a huge number of books on arranging, often easy to find in secondhand bookstores. Look for those by Constance Spry, who was a pioneer in the field. Her ideas might seem dated, but they are much the same as mine: finding beauty in unexpected materials, and making them appropriate to different kinds of rooms, and a different pace of life.

Some Thoughts on Vases

Having the right vase is key to making a successful arrangement. The reason most people don't think they can make good arrangements is because they probably haven't been using the right vases. When buying a vase you should consider its scale, proportion, and appropriateness, for instance, the size of the vase's mouth in proportion to its height and width. Too tall and narrow will be tippy. Look for tall vases with weighted bases or add some stones in the bottom. Very wide-mouthed vases will not hold flowers upright unless they're deep enough to accommodate large stems. Very short vases with fairly wide mouths work fine for little bunches. Vases that are mid-sized with straight sides (therefore wide open) can be especially difficult because there is not enough depth to support the stems, so the arrangement tends to fall wide open, or all to one side, which limits the options considerably. In a larger vase, if the opening is very small, the size of the stem that fits in may be too small to look in scale. Tiny-mouthed vases are also impossible to clean, which can make a big difference in how long an arrangement will last.

I have found that my easiest-to-use containers are odd and assorted drinking glasses I have found here and there, such as the ones on pages 63, 70, and 100. They provide a perfect height and width for a handful of anything I have grabbed on my way home. I look for good proportion when buying "real" vases as well.

Expensive vases can be prohibitive in more than price. The more you use a vase, the greater the likelihood that you will chip or break it. Buying formerly valuable, used vases, already chipped, solves that problem. Chips on the rim will usually be hidden by the arrangement anyway. Buying cheap simple vases that leave the emphasis on the arrangement is also effective. Highly designed or ornamental vases may often-times have too much personality to coexist with an arrangement.

Through the years, I have bought an embarrassing number of vases. Those I have kept and used the most are often not always the most interesting or beautiful. They are the ones that "work." When adding to my collection, I try focusing on particular shapes. What was it I just didn't have when I needed it? Just the right thing for a big top-heavy dahlia, or for a collection of something to scatter on my dinner table, or for an artisan whom I admire. And, if I have one too many, I can use it to bring flowers to a friend.

Vases and Supplies Sources

STORES

Wherever you live, there are a number of places you can look for vases, from local garden centers and flower shops to thrift and antique stores. It is a good idea to start out with inexpensive pieces until you know what works best for you. Yard sales are a good way to begin. Chips, which can be hidden by the arrangement, dramatically reduce the cost of vases that might otherwise be prohibitively expensive.

Many of the big home stores such as Crate & Barrel and Pottery Barn have a nice array of moderately priced vases. And there are a number of catalogs worth checking, such as Design Within Reach and Sundance (vase on page 60). Most of the major museums now offer vases in their gift shops and catalogs; the Museum of Modern Art in New York (MoMA Design Store) is a good example.

When I travel, I look for vases to bring home as souvenirs. They bring an added enjoyment and a special memory to each arrangement.

The first vase I can remember buying (page 126) was purchased at the glassblowing shop in Colonial Williamsburg, on a trip with my grandmother when I was about 12. I got the little vase on page 59 in a dusty antique shop in Hong Kong on my first visit to Asia.

If you are traveling to New York and want to bring home something special, there are some of my favorite places:

THE END OF HISTORY
548 Hudson Street
New York, NY 10014
212-647-7598
Mostly glass, mostly Venetian, from the 1940s and 1950s. Reasonably priced.

JONATHAN ADLER
47 Greene Street
New York, NY 10013
212 941-8950
New pottery, whimsical and very functional. Now available in shops nationwide.

MARK MCDONALD LTD.
555 Warren Street
Hudson, New York 12534
518-828-6320
One of the pioneer dealers in mid-century furniture and objects, Mark lent me many of the best vases in this book (see pages 27, 40, 44, and 120). He has an amazing collection of Scandinavian pottery among others. All are rare, valuable, and priced accordingly.

SARA
952 Lexington Avenue
New York, NY 10021
212-772-3243
Specializes in contemporary Japanese studio pottery.

TAKASHIMAYA
693 Fifth Avenue
New York, NY 10022
212 350-0100
The Christian Tortu flower shop near the main entry is always an inspiration. It has the most amazing flowers, lots of wonderful containers that really work, and some flower-arranging supplies. Worth a visit even just for looking. Be sure to go upstairs to the store's home department to see more traditional Japanese pieces.

INTERNET

The Internet has changed the way collectors shop; if you become fond of a particular type of vase, this is the way to find more. Although there isn't much romance in the process, it is addictive. eBay is the best-known place to start. If you have never bought anything on eBay before, you might want to log on with someone who has. Start slowly, read the descriptions closely, pay attention to the sizes, and keep careful notes on what you have bought. Broad categories work best but are time-consuming because there are so many listings. I check for "vases," "glass," "pottery," and other related categories.

If you get particularly interested in a certain style, designer, or maker of vases, you can also check in on the Web sites of dealers who specialize in them. Try the Internet search engine Google.com first to get an overview. A good site that has many dealers is designaddict.com.

Flower-arranging supplies are harder to find. There are many sites you can find on Google.com that sell a frightening array of handy items to help you make a stiff and tortured arrangement. However, there are some good sites as well, for example:

FLORALARTMALL.COM
For the time when you just have to try Oasis.

HOLYMTN.COM
Sells pin frogs (Kenzans).

SAMADHI-JAPANESE-ARTS.COM
Also offers Kenzans, plus traditional Japanese scissors which you can keep on your hand while arranging.

A Few Good Plants to Grow

Although it is not necessary to have a garden to supply material for arranging, if you are a gardener, you might like to try growing some of the following. They are all quite easy; just give them full sun, good soil, and protection from the wind. Having an area only for cutting is best so that you won't hesitate to cut all the flowers. I grow them in with my vegetables, which have the same cultural requirements and also provide inspiration for cutting.

TENDER BULBS

If you have a deep frost in your area, tender bulbs must be dug and stored in a cool, dry place over the winter. This extra work is worth it, as the growing part is so easy.

ACIDANTHERAS

These relatives of the gladiola are delicate and loose and highly fragrant. They increase rapidly, so you can start with just a few and have hundreds within a few years. Since they bloom quite quickly after planting, I put them out at two-week intervals through the end of June to have a continuous supply.

DAHLIAS

The cactus-flowered types of dahlias are my favorites; I find the pompon varieties stiff and tight. Not all the fancy ones are reliable about making it through storage, so order a few new ones each year, just in case. Some real show stoppers are papageno, tropic sun, Margaret Duross, rip city, poppers, and purple gem.

GALTONIAS

Rather like a tuberose without the fragrance, galtonias are worth growing for their graceful form, long-lasting flowers, and the green-tinted variety "viridiflora."

HYMENOCALLISES

Known as Peruvian daffodils or ismenes, these are like huge exotic daffodils. A brief but amazing moment. Fragrant. I like the "Sulphur Queen" variety.

ORNITHOGALUM SANDERSIAE

Although each bulb may produce only one flower, its longevity makes up for the lack of others. It can be a period of weeks from the time these produce their strangely beautiful buds until the flowers fade. Unlike dahlias, they survive winter storage with very few losses.

TUBEROSES

These are one of the rare examples in a flower that has not been destroyed by a hybrid double form, which is equal to the single form in fragrance and long vase life.

HARDY BULBS

ALLIUMS

There are endless different alliums, with bloom times from spring through fall. Some are huge, some tiny. Mostly lavenders and blues, they also come in yellow, pink, green, and white. All are easy to grow. My favorites include azureum, flavum, pulchellum, and triquetrum.

DAFFODILS

There are some daffodils I grow just for cutting, because I think some are too fancy for naturalizing, some too tiny. The double forms such as Tahiti and golden ducat are among the former, and the little bulbocodiums such as golden bells and conspicuous, the latter. The bulbocodiums are very late to bloom, so be careful not to dig them up by mistake. They look especially great, with a bit of foliage, in one of the *Kenzans* that comes in its own little bowl.

TULIPS

Tulips are just about perfect. The different varieties will provide a very long bloom period, and you can plant something else right over them once they are finished. Although most are listed as annuals, many will return, with fewer smaller blossoms. Purchasing tulip bulbs expressly for cutting alters the selection process. I go for colors I would not be likely to put in my garden where they look too exotic or shockingly bright: the feathered and streaked ones like tangerine beauty, flair, Princess Irene, banja luka, flaming parrot, golden artist, and rococo. They cut easily and hold well. I love the peony-flowering forms such as Mount Tacoma and orange princess. The little species types such as clusianas and chrysantha will perennialize better, so plant them in a place where they won't be disturbed or be overwhelmed by competing growth.

ANNUALS

COSMOS

These are easy to grow and long blooming if you keep cutting them, so don't be timid— cut big hunks of stems to keep the plants from getting lanky and floppy. I prefer the orange and red "sulphureus" varieties such as "bright lights." Be sure to avoid the short bedding-out varieties; they have almost no stems.

GOURDS

Gourds take up huge amounts of room, so try wrestling them up on a fence or trellis where they will benefit from staying off the ground. The large types make a great fast-growing shade cover as long as the support is sturdy. Start plenty of seeds indoors and don't put them out until the ground is warm, as they have a distressing tendency to rot until well established.

LISIANTHUSES

Impossible to grow yourself from seed, and difficult to find as plants, these are worth seeking out, as the flowers last so long when cut. Most of the plants offered in garden centers are the short ones, which don't cut well at all. Look for echo and Heidi varieties.

NASTURTIUMS

Probably the easiest annual to grow, nasturtiums taste as good as they look. The leaves add a great peppery flavor to salads. I like to grow a few different kinds, because the flowers have great colors, and the flavors have subtle differences. Empress of India, a deep orange flower, has the most beautiful leaves: large and blue green. That with the deep red of the variety mahogany makes a great combination.

NICOTIANA LANGSDORFII

This member of the tobacco family doesn't have the expected fragrance, but it produces constant sprays of delicate green bells. It needs to be cut often because once it goes to seed it will stop blooming and get ratty looking. It looks great in a flower border.

RUDBECKIAS

Try the annual rudbeckias, which bloom all summer. The flowers are larger and especially interesting when in bud. Indian summer and prairie sun are yellow, chimchiminee is a mix with some remarkable brown blossoms, and green wizard is, yes, green.

SUNFLOWERS

Every year there is a new variety of sunflowers being offered. The branching types continue to produce flowers as they are cut. Growing sunflowers is an especially good project for children because they have big seeds that are easy to handle and never fail to germinate.

SWEET PEAS

I grow sweet peas on my garden fence, planting as many varieties as I can fit; they are all great.

ZINNIAS

Pick your color; zinnias come in every one. Look for varieties with long stems, such as pumila and pulcino, as many have now been bred as short stocky plants for massing in flowerbeds. The older varieties such as cut and come again are still great, but they can be prone to mildew. The newer binary hybrids have better mildew resistance and larger blooms. All are easy to grow from seed, right in the ground.

SELF-SOWING ANNUALS

Some flowers come back year after year if you let them go to seed and learn to recognize the seedlings in the spring. Just in case of an especially brutal winter, I save some seed in the fall for planting by hand in the spring. If they make the winter, though, I find the self-sown plants will usually be the healthier.

BUPLEUREUMS

Odd plants that resemble euphorbias and provide the much sought-after color chartreuse. Used as filler by professional florists, they are fine on their own as well.

CENTAUREA CYANUS

Bachelor buttons are ageless, and now, with new colors of dark intensity, modern as well.

They can get a bit floppy, but that can be avoided by cutting long stems so the plants get bushier. As soon as the weather gets hot they will fade out, so plant lots and cut them hard, then pull them out and plant something that blooms late, such as one of the tender bulbs.

COREOPSIS TINCTORIA

These meadow plants are usually a combination of deep red and yellow. I prize the occasional all-red ones, but to get them reliably you need to buy the pure seed from time to time.

EMILIA JAVANICA

Known as tassel flowers, these little puffs of red or orange on long stems are easy to use; arrangements work well with just a few or a big bunch.

EUPHORBIA MARGINATA

Snow on the mountains are variegated foliage plants. In addition to being good on their own, when the foliage is used with big, white and greeny white flowers, such as Hydrangea macrophylla alba, they provide a bold accent.

NIGELLAS

Love-in-a-mists are one of the all-time great flowers for arranging; both the flowers and seedpods are fascinating. They go dormant when the weather gets hot but by then, there is much else to choose from.

TALINUM PANICULATUM

Jewels of Opar always get attention as they are seldom seen. Although the flowers are tiny, there are so many of them, on airy sprays, they make a big impression. The flowers are followed by shiny little seeds, prolonging their ornamental life for weeks in a vase.

PERENNIALS AND GRASSES

ASCLEPIAS TUBEROSA

Remarkably easy to grow, these native wildflowers make surprisingly good cuts. Because they are generally fairly rare in the wild, I do not encourage picking them that way. Grow your own; the plants will multiply and even seed around if given the chance. Don't bother trying to transplant them, the taproot is too deep and they seldom survive.

BELAMCANDAS

Very much like an iris, until they bloom, blackberry lilies are charming and reliable and the seedpods and flowers make equally great cuts. The common name comes from the look of the seeds, which are prolific and germinate readily if scattered where you want more to grow.

CHASMANTHIUM LATIFOLIUM

There is hardly a grass that does not produce a seed head suitable for cutting. But if you were going to specifically plant one, this would be my suggestion. Tolerant of almost any kind of abuse, it looks attractive in the garden as well as in a vase. I have planted it as a short hedge with great success. If you want an arrangement of it to last indefinitely, try making one without any water.

EGYPTIAN ONIONS

I have never figured out the Latin name for these funny onions, which curl at the top and produce bulblets shooting out in all directions. They make a great gift as, when the arrangement has faded, the bulblets can be planted.

HOSTAS

These are an old standby in a shady garden. With so many varieties to choose from, I am always surprised not to see them in arrangements more often. Try using the new leaves that are just unfurling. The flowers are also excellent for cutting. Royal standard, a white-flowered variety, is fragrant as well.

IRISES

The best irises for cutting are the good old germanicas, which also have the widest color range. A new range of twice-blooming varieties really does bloom again in the fall. Not many colors are offered yet, but I expect they will be. Always buy big strong irises in pots from your local garden center. Resist the fabulous photos in the catalogs; the mail-order and packaged rhizomes have a very high failure rate.

KNIPHOFIAS

Marginally hardy in northeastern gardens, these plants do best with good drainage and hot summers. Their common name, red hot poker, sums it up. Some, such as Percy's pride, wayside flame, and Bressingham comet, have colors that seem to glow from within. Just one in a vase, with a single leaf, is stunning. For the best selection I have found, see Digging Dog Nursery, in the Sources.

LILIES

Naturally, I prefer the unusual, species forms; try henryi or lancifolium. For the fragrant types, the larger trumpet varieties such as African queen are hard to resist.

SCABIOSAS

These are reliable plants with long-lasting long-stemmed flowers that have an old-fashioned look. "Butterfly blue" is the current favorite.

SOLIDAGO "FIREWORKS"

This ornamental goldenrod is best in bud and lasts a very long time.

TREE PEONIES

Hardier than anyone thought, tress peonies are now becoming widely available and far less expensive. They have amazing buds, amazing flowers, and gorgeous leaves. They can now be found in pots at most garden centers, which is the best way to buy them, as mail-order stock can be very small.

SHRUBS

DOGWOODS

Mixing the variegated leaves of the yellow or red twig types of dogwood with branches of tardivas just opening is a classic.

HYDRANGEAS

As many as you can fit in: hortensias, tardivas (fragrant!), peegees, and the very hardy Annabelles, which are an especially great green when the bloom has gone a bit old.

SALIX SPP.

There are many willows that have interesting branch colors and unusual leaves in addition to their better-known furry buds. Try Chaenomeloides (pinkish-silver) or Melanostachys (black) for interesting buds, and alba vitellina (yellow) or britensis (coral) for intensely colored stems in the spring. These plants get huge but can be cut right to the ground each spring, which also produces the best color.

WEEDS

You can always let one area of your property go wild. Mowing once or twice a year in March and June will keep most noxious stuff such as bittersweet and bindweed at bay. You might be surprised at what has lain dormant in your soil for years upon years. I have seen asters, butterfly weed, and black-eyed Susans appear after a while. And with them come butterflies, fireflies, and birds. Planting a few native fruiting shrubs such as *Viburnum dentatum* or *trilobum* will increase the wildlife and add to your cutting inventory. There are many named selections if you want extra bloom potential. Make sure not to buy nonfruiting varieties such as *Vibernum opulus sterile*. Also, resist the urge to irrigate; it only encourages the weeds you don't want.

Plant Sources

You can find almost any plant on the Internet through Google.com but you might not get the best quality. Still, it is fun to experiment, and the following are some of the best.

BRENT AND BECKY'S BULBS
7463 Heath Trail
Gloucester, VA 23061
(877) 661-2852
www.brentandbeckysbulbs.com

DIGGING DOG NURSERY
P.O. Box 471
Albion, CA 95410
(707) 937-1130
www.diggingdog.com

ROCKY FORD GOURDS
P.O. Box 222
Cygnet, OH 42413
(419) 655-2152
www.wcnet.org/~ackerman/

SEED SAVERS EXCHANGE
3076 North Winn Road
Decorah, IA 52101
(563) 382-5990
www.seedsavers.org

**SELECT SEEDS,
ANTIQUE FLOWERS**
180 Stickney Hill Road
Union, CT 06076
(860) 684-9310
www.selectseeds.com

SWAN ISLAND DAHLIAS
P.O. Box 700
Canby, OR 97013
(800) 503-266-8768
www.dahlias.com

Pronunciation Guide

Acer (ā´ser)

Allium schoenoprasum
(al´i-um skoyn-ō-prah´sum)

Amaranthus retroflexus
(am-à-ran´thus re-trō-fleks´us)

Ampelopsis brevipedunculata
(am-pel-op´sis brev-i-ped-unk-ū-lā´tà)

Anemone coronaria (à-nem´ō-nē kôr-ō-nā´rē-à)

Arctium minus (ark´tē-um mī´nus)

Arisaema triphyllum (ar-i-sē´mà trī-fil´um)

Asclepias syriaca (as-klē´pi-as si-ri-ā´kà)

Berberis thunbergii (bēr´bēr-is thun-bēr´ji-ī)

Beta vulgaris (bē´tà vul-gar´is)

Castanea mollissima (kas-tā´nē-à mol-is´i-mà)

Chaenomeles speciosa
(kē-nom´e-lēz spē-si-ō´sà)

Chamaecyparis pisifera filifera aurea variegata
(kam-e-sip´à-ris pi-si´fēr-à fi-lif´ēr-à ã´rē-à vãr-i-e-gā´tà)

Coccoloba uvifera (kō-kō-lō´bà ū-vi´fēr-à)

Cornus racemosa (kôr´nus ra-se-mō´sà)

Cornus sericea (kôr´nus se-rē´sē-à)

Cucurbita pepo (kŭ-kēr´bi-tà pe´pō)

Cynara scolymus
(sī-nà´rà or sin´à-rà sko´li-mus)

Dolichos lablab (dō-lee´kōs làb´làb)

Equisetum hyemale (ek-wi-sē´tum hī-e-māl´)

Euonymous alatus (ū-on´i-mus à-lā´tus)

Fagus grandifolia (fā´gus gran-di-fō´lē-à)

Hamamelis virginiana
(ham-à-mē´lis vēr-jin-i-ā´nà)

Helianthus anuus (hē-li-an´thus an´ū-us)

Houttuynia cordata (hoo-tī´nē-à kor-dā´tà)

Ilex verticillata (ī´leks ver-ti-si-lā´ta)

Liquidambar styraciflua
(lik-wid-am´bär stī-ra-se-floo´à)

Lycopersicon esculentum cerasiforme
(lī-kō-pēr´si-kon es-kū-len´tum sēr-à´-si-form)

Maclura pomifera (mà-kloo´rà pō-mif´ēr-à)

Malus (mà´lus)

Petroselinum crispum
(pe-tro-se-lī´num kris´pum)

Phalaris arundinacea picta
(fàl´à-ris à-run-di-nā´cē-à pik´tà)

Phaseolus (fà-se´ō-lus)

Physalis alkekengi (fis´à-lis àl-ke-ken´jē)

Phytolacca americana (fi-tō-lak´à à-mer-i-kā´nà)

Pinus thunbergii (pī´nus thun-bēr´ji-ī)

Pyracantha (pī-rà-kan´thà)

Pyrus communis (pī´rus ko-mū´nis)

Quercus (kwēr´kus)

Rhus typhina (rus tī-fī´nà)

Rosa
multiflora (rō´zà mul-ti-flō´rà)
rugosa (rō´zà ru-gō´sà)
sevillana (rō´zà se-vil-à´nà)

Rubus occidentalis (roo´bus ok-si-den-tā´lis)

Rubus odoratus (roo´bus ō-do-rà´tis)

Rumex crispus (rŭ´meks kris´pus)

Salix alba 'vitellina' (sā´liks al´bà vit-e-lē´nà)

Salix chaenomeloides
(sā´liks kē-nom´e-loy-dēz)

Schoenoplectus subtermindis
(skoy-nō-plek´tus sub-tēr-min´dis)

Tropaeolum majus (trō-pē´ō-lum mā´jus)

Vaccinium corymbosum
(vak-sin´i-um kôr-im-bō´sum)

Virbinum dentatum (vī-bēr´num den-tā´tum)

Bibliography

THERE ARE three types of horticulture or botanical reference works that I turn to: one to use for identifying plants I don't know; one in which to find out more about plants whose names I do know; and one for exploring specialized subjects. I have commented on those I use, or recommend, the most.

Adams, George. *Birdscaping Your Garden*. Emmaus, Pa.: Rodale Press, 1994.

Britton, Nathaniel Lord, and Hon. Addison Brown. *An Illustrated Flora of the Northern United States and Canada*. New York: Dover Publications, 1970. *A comprehensive resource for native plant identification. The book I turn to when I can't figure out what something is from more colorful and portable sources.*

Coffey, Timothy. *The History and Folklore of Northern American Wildflowers*. New York: Facts on File, 1993.

Coombes, Allen J. *Dictionary of Plant Names*. Portland, Ore.: Timber Press, 1994.

Dirr, Michael. *Manual of Woody Landscape Plants*. Champagne, Ill.: Stipes Publishing, 1990. *The bible of the landscape industry, with very complete information on just about every plant available to the trade and Dirr's candid opinions. Excellent glossary and section on morphology. Michael Dirr is a hero to us all.*

Everett, Thomas H. *The New York Botanical Garden Illustrated Encyclopedia of Horticulture*. New York: Garland Publishing, 1981. *Mostly cultural information for garden and house plants. Especially useful for looking up something obscure.*

Foster, Steven, and Roger Caras. *Venomous Animals and Poisonous Plants*. New York: Houghton Mifflin, 1994.

Grimm, William Carey. *The Illustrated Book of Wildflowers and Shrubs*. Harrisburg, Pa.: Stackpole Books, 1993.

Harlow, William M. *Fruit Key and Twing Key*. New York: Dover Publications, 1954.

Huxley, Anthony, Mark Griffiths, and Margot Levy, eds. *The New Royal Horticultural Society Dictionary of Gardening*. New York: The Stockton Press, 1992. *The current standard reference. An immense work that can be difficult to use due to little or no cross referencing. Expensive, too, but worth more than most others combined.*

Levine, Carol. *A Guide to Wildflowers in Winter*. New Haven: Yale University Press, 1995.

Neal, Bill. *Gardener's Latin*. Chapel Hill, N.C.: Algonquin Books of Chapel Hill, 1992.

New Pronouncing Dictionary of Plant Names. Chicago: Florists' Publishing Company, 1964. *A wonderful little pamphlet, now in its over-twentieth printing, that is hard to find. Ask your local garden center to call 800-621-5727 to order; they are cheap. Even better, find an old used one. It had the best cover and might cost even less.*

Niering, William A., and Nancy C. Olmstead. *The Audubon Society Field Guide to North American Wildflowers*. New York: Alfred A. Knopf, 1983. *For identifying plants in the field. I like that this guide has photos instead of line drawings. The big failing is that the Latin names are not printed with the pictures. I wish it covered more plants; I wouldn't mind the extra bulk.*

1995 Ethnobotanical Catalogue of Seeds (Catalogue #56). La Honda, Cal.: J.L. Hudson, Seedsman, Jan. 1995. *No pictures, but highly informative, with an individual approach.*

Phillips, Roger, and Martin Rix. *The Random House Book of Vegetables*. New York: Random House, 1993. *Not the first book to buy about growing vegetables, but irresistible once you're hooked. Information on many unusual varieties, and luscious photographs.*

Plantes sauvages des villes, des champs (et en bordure des chemins). Saint-Augustin, Quebec: Fleurbec, 1983. *One of a great set of books, even if your French is terrible. Good photos for identification; good coverage of commonly neglected species, especially grasses. The companion seashore wild-plant guide has no equal that I have found.*

Shigo, Alex L. *100 Tree Myths*. Durham, N.H.: Shigo and Trees, Assoc., 1993. *A remarkable book by a man who has influenced tremendously the way trees are maintained. Unfortunately, it is difficult to read because it assumes a certain knowledge, and the presentation is scrambled.*

Staff of the L. H. Bailey Hortorium. *Hortus Third*. New York: Macmillan Publishing Company, 1976. *The old standby for checking correctness of botanical nomenclature, upstaged at this time by the newer New Royal Horticultural Society Dictionary (see above). Certainly not a neccesity for the library, but one tends to have to have it anyway.*

Stearn, William T. *Stearn's Dictionary of Plant Names for Gardeners*. London: Cassell Publishers Limited, 1992. *The origins and meanings of plants' names; it is difficult to read just one entry.*

Stokes, Donald W. *A Guide to Nature in Winter*. Boston: Little, Brown & Co., 1976.